SEVEN
MONTANAS

SEVEN
MONTANAS

A Journey in Search of the Soul of the Treasure State

EDNOR THERRIAULT

TWODOT®

GUILFORD, CONNECTICUT
HELENA, MONTANA

A · T W O D O T® · B O O K

An imprint and registered trademark of The Rowman & Littlefield Publishing Group, Inc.
4501 Forbes Blvd., Ste. 200
Lanham, MD 20706
www.rowman.com

Distributed by NATIONAL BOOK NETWORK

British Library Cataloguing in Publication Information available

Library of Congress Cataloging-in-Publication Data available

ISBN 978-1-4930-4160-2 (hardcover)
ISBN 978-1-4930-4161-9 (e-book)

♾™ The paper used in this publication meets the minimum requirements of American National Standard for Information Sciences—Permanence of Paper for Printed Library Materials, ANSI/NISO Z39.48-1992.

FOR SHANNON

Always a welcome sight at the end of the road

State Route 28 tops a rise on the Flathead
Indian Reservation and drops into the Little
Bitterroot Valley, just west of Kalispell.

CONTENTS

ACKNOWLEDGMENTS

Thanks, first off, to my editor, Erin Turner. Your belief in not only my idea for this book but in my ability to pull it off was the fuel I needed once I realized I'd bitten off way more than I could chew. Thank you for reminding me to chew thoroughly.

Thank you to my friend, poet and storyteller Philip Burgess. Your unabashed life-long romance with Montana was contagious, and your knowledge of the state's history—and the Native American history that preceded it—was invaluable. I appreciate your occasional reminders to take this stuff seriously, damn your eyes.

To my friends across the state, old and new, who offered this nosy traveler a bunk for the night, I thank you. Next time I'll remember to bring my guitar.

Clouds build over a ranch on Highway 181,
just south of the Fort Belknap Reservation.

To Tim Ryan, my copilot of the inner cosmos, the Neal to my Jack, my brother from another mother (hi, Alice!)—you introduced me to the beauty and depth of Native American culture and the proper perspective for living on this planet.

To the people who live and work in Colstrip, the tribal members from Rocky Boy's, the Gustafson family, JFlo, Big Mike, Chips, and everyone else I spoke to for this book, thank you for your honesty and openness. There could be no Seven Montanas without you.

I also offer a heartfelt thank you to the staff at the Montana Historical Society Research Library.

Finally, thank you to my wife Shannon for dealing with my absence, my presence, my deadlines, my moods and my stealing the covers. Your contributions to this book were much appreciated.

INTRODUCING THE UNITED STATES OF MONTANA

STARTING A BOOK WITH A BUNCH OF DRY STATISTICS is a sure way to make the reader's eyes glaze over, but I'll take my chances and give you just a couple here: Montana has 151,209 miles of roadway. Of that, fewer than 7,000 miles comprise the paved streets that run through a city or town. From the sleek, banked ribbon of I-90 that can carry you from the Pacific to the Atlantic, to the rutted gravel county roads, straight as a guitar string, that crisscross the farmland in much of the state, most of the roadways in Montana are out in the open spaces, leading from town to town, but more importantly, from one person to the next. After all, what determines the personality of any state more than its people?

I won't waste our time, though, by trying to conjure up an image of the typical Montanan. There is no such thing. We are as individual as the rocks in a mountain stream, and it's a mistake to assign regional identities or any kind of common personality type based on what part of the state we call home. By that criterion I could have called this book *One Million Montanas*. I think you get my point.

There are, however, certain qualities that are peculiar to each of Montana's different areas, and the characteristics of each region—its history, topography, main economic engine, and other factors—give it a unique set of challenges and opportunities. That's where each area's people combine to create their part of the bigger picture—a six-piece mosaic, if you will—of the state of Montana.

The sheer physical variety of the Treasure State's landscape plays a big part in its multiple personalities, from the verdant mountain forests of the northwest to the arid, desert-like badlands of the southeast, and the wild mix of geology in between. When it comes to natural splendor, Montana has more than its share. You want mountains?

The geology and plant life between Cooke City and Yellowstone Park are just a hint of the rugged beauty in this part of the state.

There are more than a hundred mountain ranges in the state, containing dozens of peaks reaching 10,000 feet or more. All these mountains create watersheds, and Montana's thousands of miles of rivers and streams feed into

The Western Meadowlark is Montana's state bird, and its song can be heard in all six regions.
Photo © Jonathan Qualben

hundreds of lakes and reservoirs, providing irrigation for millions of acres of agriculture, and endless recreation opportunities in every part of the state.

Then there's Montana's fauna. This is the wildlife photographer's mecca. The hunter's valhalla. We have grizzlies in the west, pronghorns in the east, trumpeter swans in the south, and prairie dogs all over the place. Montana boasts the largest number of mammal species in the continental U.S., and the management of all that wildlife presents a series of ever-evolving issues that have a different focus in every region, some affecting several regions. For example, the iconic Montana buffalo, which numbered in the millions before being hunted to near-extinction only 150 years ago, are making a comeback statewide. But at what cost? Tribes would love to reestablish buffalo herds on the reservations, while cattle ranchers would love to see the buffalo—which carry a cow-threatening disease called brucellosis—appear nowhere outside the back of a nickel.

Trying to pin down the different characteristics of each of Montana's disparate territories isn't an easy task, and there are a lot of moving parts to this machine.

For the purpose of convenience and organization, I've divvied up Montana into the six classic tourism regions: Missouri River Country, Custer Country, Yellowstone Country, Gold West Country, Glacier Country and Russell Country. Every one of the six regions has a long list of wonderful attributes, but they also wrestle with their own set of conservation and natural resource issues, whether it's culling wolf populations in Yellowstone Country or proposing logging projects in the Kootenai National Forest in Glacier Country or allowing the expansion of the Rosebud coal mine in Custer Country.

Climate change is a common enemy, a proven threat to the West in the form of intensifying and larger wildfires sweeping through forests during a fire season that seems to get longer each year. August in Montana, which used to mean state fairs and peak tourism, now means smoky skies and respirators. While the fires themselves cause death and destruction mostly in the forested west, the whole state deals with the smoke. During one day in Montana's 2018 fire season, all 56 counties were suffering degraded air quality from forest fires in the western U.S. and Montana.

Montana is also shaped to some degree from outside influences. Thirteen million visitors per year come to Montana, drawn by our world class trout fishing, big game hunting, rafting, camping, hiking, and some of the best skiing in North America. Cottage industries supporting all kinds of outdoor pursuits continue to pop up like morel mushrooms after a forest fire, providing 53,000 jobs a year. Those jobs generate $181 million in state and local taxes (again with the statistics), while lowering the taxes on each Montana household by an average of $426, just about enough to cover that household's energy bill for January.

One million people, one million stories. But wait, the title of the book is not *Six Montanas*. Where is the seventh Montana? That's the one that doesn't exist yet. It's the Montana that lies somewhere up the road, just beyond the reach of the headlights. It's the Montana we hope to see, the one we need to see as we creep deeper into the twenty-first century. Our concerns are many. We want to protect the environment while improving the economy. We need to confront the issues that are destroying lives and families on Montana's Indian reservations. We must find ways to provide good-paying jobs and fulfilling careers for future generations, so they don't have to flee the state to make a decent living. The importance of these and dozens of other challenges facing Montana shifts, depending on whom you're talking to, and what part of the state they call home.

This book is about those seven different Montanas—though there are probably more. But there's also one Montana, the one we all fell in love with. It's the one that is endless miles of open land and the sweet smell of prairie grasses. Its snow-capped mountain peaks that reach to the heavens, and an expanse of deep blue sky that stretches from one horizon to the other. Being a Montanan also implies having the strong backbone of pioneer spirit that drew so many of our antecedents from points back east hundreds of years ago, or perhaps across a land bridge from the west a couple of ice ages ago. Millions of visitors from all over the world feel the pull every year and return again and again, sometimes staying for good. Ask a million people what Montana means to them and you'll get a million answers. Hopefully, this book contains a few that you haven't heard before.

Oliver Wendell Holmes
quote lettered on the side
of a garage in Saco along
Highway 2.

*The Burlington Northern Santa Fe parallels Highway 2 on the
Hi-Line for hundreds of miles across the northern tier of Montana.*

MISSOURI RIVER COUNTRY

IT'S EASY TO LOOK AT A MAP OF MONTANA and point to the northeast corner and say there's nothing there. After all, there are only a couple of state parks, no interstate freeways, and the hills big enough to be called mountains can be counted on one hand. But what a map doesn't show is the people who live there, and their connection to the land. Nor does a map convey a kind of beauty you just can't see until you're in the middle of it.

*Fort Union Trading Post
National Historic Site as
seen from the guard tower.*

These broad prairies are scattered with geological remnants of ancient seas, with regions of dramatic cliffs and canyons known as badlands. Agriculture has driven the economy here for generations, although oil and gas production from the Bakken Shale Formation has had a major, if inconsistent, impact on the region for decades.

Agricultural economy is affected largely by factors outside of the region, so those in the eastern part of the state who make their living off the land largely ignore the cultural or social upheavals that take place in the bumpy west. The main thing that dictates their livelihoods and their day-to-day existence is the land. They have weather and climate to contend with, but the land rarely changes. Ranchers and farmers in this part of the state tend to take the long view—while they're used to extreme weather cycles and market fluctuations, it can sometimes be uninformed decisions emanating from Helena that complicate their livelihoods.

This is big, rugged country that demands self-reliance. It was the last part of the state to be settled, as pioneers from the east moved right through it on their way to the resource-laden mountains of the west. This settlement pattern is a demographic oddity that's peculiar to Montana, as most of the West was settled east-to-west. The hardiest folk eventually did put down roots here, though, and their descendants still work the same land, albeit with modern methods and technology that makes life on the plains much less of a hardship.

Fire start (the origin point of a wildfire or prescribed burn) near the confluence of the Missouri and Yellowstone Rivers.

Oil rigs working the Baaken Shale Field in Missouri Country.

Missouri River Country is also home to Fort Peck Indian reservation, home of the Assiniboine and Nakota tribes. It's located just northeast of Fort Peck Lake, a sprawling, many-fingered body of water that spreads out endlessly into the impressive Charles M. Russell National Wildlife Refuge, a stunning landscape that could give a National Park a run for its money.

Up north, within an hour of the Canadian border, this area is traversed by the storied Hi-Line, a series of small towns dotting the U.S. Route 2 that runs alongside the Burlington Northern Santa Fe Railroad for much of Montana. The Hi-Line, and Missouri River Country in general, might just epitomize the big sky of Big Sky Country. There's something about being out there, with the wind blowing across a snow-blanketed prairie, with nothing but flat horizon as far as the eye can see, that's pure and powerful. The sheer scale and distances here really can give you some perspective on your place in the world. The people who live in Missouri River Country, or grew up here and moved on, know it. If the lack of green patches and topographic squiggles on a map lead you to believe there's nothing out here, you're dead wrong. This is striking, handsome country and it takes a dyed-in-the-wool Montanan to appreciate it and call it home.

Native grasses at Bowdoin
National Wildlife Refuge support
dozens of species of birds.

DISCOVERING BOWDOIN

ANY BIRDER WORTH HIS BUSHNELLS KNOWS that Montana has more than its share of excellent birdwatching opportunities. From the harlequin ducks in Glacier Park to the snow geese at Freezeout Lake, you can stuff your Instagram with endless photos of vast number of feathered specimens from hummingbirds to bald eagles that fly the Big Sky. In the west, the popular Teller Wildlife Refuge and Lee Metcalf Wildlife Refuge lie within 20 minutes of each other in the Bitterroot Valley, and in the Missouri Breaks the massive C. M. Russell Wildlife Refuge surrounds Fort Peck Lake. Ask any Montana birdwatching enthusiast to name her favorite, however, and Bowdoin National Wildlife Refuge (BNWR) will be mentioned time and again. Judging by several ornithological and environmental criteria, Bowdoin may be the most important of them all.

Located seven miles northeast of Malta on the Hi-Line, 50 miles from the Canadian border, BNWR is an out-of-the-way destination that features a vast number of species not only of birds, but prairie mammals and a few megafauna as well. It's one of Montana's great watering holes, drawing 236 species of birds and serving as an important way station for migratory flocks on the Pacific and Central Flyways. Shorebirds, waterfowl, grassland birds—virtually every species that nests in or migrates through Montana can be seen here.

Lake Bowdoin, the 4,000-acre centerpiece of the 15,551-acre refuge, wasn't always a pothole lake that pulls in birds year-round. Fifteen thousand years ago, an ice sheet broke loose from Canada and migrated, moving a five-mile-wide channel of water—what's now the Missouri River—50 miles south. The oxbow that was left behind formed a series of lakes known today as the Bowdoin Complex. Other refuges on the 14-site prairie pothole chain include Black Coulee, Creedman Coulee, Hewitt Lake and Lake Thibadeau. The complex sprawls over 84,724 acres of rolling prairie.

Before human settlement, Lake Bowdoin was a catch basin for floods and heavy spring runoff, causing the level of the lake to fluctuate year to year. By the 1800s the lake had become an important water source for cattle being moved through the area, and the grasslands began to pay the price. Overgrazing was trashing the terrain, and

conservation-minded sportsmen began to take notice. The area was popular with hunters, and by the early 1920s the Milk River Gun Club had erected a massive lodge on the lake shore. The Club offered a proposal to the U.S. Congress: they would protect the land, enforce game laws, and keep poachers away if they were granted 80 acres of land surrounding the Club. Although the bill passed the House and Senate, it was nixed by President Wilson, who may have already begun to see the area's value as a preserve rather than a hunting ground. Shortly after Wilson's veto the Club moved to Malta, but the building still remains.

Bowdoin National Wildlife Preserve was established in 1936, providing both salt- and fresh-water habitat for migratory birds. As the twentieth century marched on, man's encroachment on several species' habitats was taking its toll. The Canada goose, ubiquitous today, was nearly extirpated in the early- to mid-twentieth century due to over-hunting and habitat loss. Thanks to habitat improvement efforts at Bowdoin and other refuges such as Medicine Lake, the birds' numbers began to rebound by the early 1940s. The staff at Bowdoin also began incubating and hatching eggs, relocating the goslings to other prairie wetland refuges. Reintroduction of the Canada goose remains one of BNWR's biggest accomplishments.

Today, drivers, bikers, and intrepid hikers can tour Bowdoin year-round on the 15-mile two-track that circles the lake. It's a well-placed path that comes close enough to bird habitat to allow for great views, but not close enough to disturb the birds. Waterfowl such as double-crested cormorants, American white pelicans, grebes, northern pintails, and other ducks are scattered all over the lake. With a decent zoom lens, you can also capture crisp images of wading shorebirds such as great blue herons, white-faced ibis, black-crowned night herons and more. The lake is also a favorite haunt of seagull species like Franklin's, ring-billed and the California gull. Blackbirds (both red-winged and yellow-headed), western meadowlarks and other passerine species fill the air with song, adding a whimsical soundtrack to the experience.

Bowdoin has plenty to offer for a wide variety of winged species. The area's native grasses are supremely high quality, enough to draw Sprague's pipit and the Baird's sparrow, some very discerning birds.

Wildlife buffs can find several terrestrial species in the refuge complex, from rabbits and skunks to larger animals like bobcats and white-tailed deer. Pronghorn, the sleek speedster of the Eastern prairie, abound. After the Bowdoin Migratory Waterfowl Refuge was established by President Franklin D. Roosevelt in 1936, hunting was verboten, and the pronghorn is one species whose very existence in this area of Montana can be partially credited to the protection of Bowdoin. Their population had dropped to a mere seven individuals on the BNWR in the 1940s, but today counts on the refuge range between 100 and 150.

One thing you'll notice right away on the auto trail are the large patches of white interspersed among the grasses around the lake. What look like the sugar-white sands of a Gulf Coast beach are actually alkaline deposits. Although the water levels of Lake Bowdoin are kept relatively constant by the Milk River diversion from Dodson, there's still evaporation to contend with. During the parched summer months up to 40 inches of water can evaporate from the lake. As the lakeshore recedes, it leaves behind sodium, calcium, magnesium and other salts leached from the water. The wind dissipates a lot of it, though, and during high water flows in the spring it's mostly flushed away.

A small visitor's center is located at the head of the auto trail, and the staff are knowledgeable and helpful about where and when to observe wildlife all over the refuge. A large whiteboard just inside the door bears the entries of dozens of visitors who log the rare and elusive species of birds they've identified. This birder's paradise doesn't see a lot of traffic, rewarding visitors with a relaxed, peaceful experience while they mark specific species off their checklist, or just take it all in and enjoy the broad spectrum of animals cavorting in this beautiful grassland prairie and the inviting waters of its lake. Prime animal activity happens around sunrise and sunset, so headquartering in nearby Malta would afford quick access from the comfort of a hotel.

It may surprise some that the seemingly empty expanse of prairie in much of Missouri River Country could contain such a largesse of riparian beauty, but the Bowdoin National Wildlife Refuge is just one example of the various natural wonders that appear in Montana's northeast. It's a must-see for the birding buff who wants to witness one of the state's biggest concentrations and widest variety of birds.

KID CURRY'S HAPPY PLACE

Oh, give me land, lots of land under starry skies above
Don't fence me in
Let me ride through the wide-open country that I love
Don't fence me in
"DON'T FENCE ME IN" by Cole Porter

WHILE THE LYRICS OF COLE PORTER'S COWBOY CLASSIC might conjure visions of the expansive vistas afforded by Montana's northeast quadrant, many of Missouri River Country's inhabitants in the late 1800s saw these wide-open spaces as the perfect place to hole up while evading the bounty hunters and law enforcement types who wanted nothing better than to bring them to justice for their crimes. From "Dutch" Henry Ieuch to George "Big Nose" Parrott, scores of horse thieves, cattle rustlers and train robbers of the Old West chose to hide out in the sparsely populated territory north of the Missouri River, bounded by Canada and the Dakotas. They were less concerned with being fenced in than by being locked up.

The Wild West outlaw is such an enduring character in folklore and popular culture that it comes as a bit of a surprise that his heyday lasted only about thirty years during the main expansion of pioneers and settlers into the west. Many of these mounted miscreants traveled the infamous Outlaw Trail, which ran from Saskatchewan, Canada, through Wyoming, Utah, Colorado and Arizona, on into Mexico. In Missouri River Country, horse thieves and cattle rustlers moved freely back and forth between Canada and Montana, crossing the porous border between Saskatchewan and Sheridan County, north of Plentywood. The trail, more a series of hideouts than an actual path, runs westward from there, passing through Scobey before turning south to meander through Wyoming, Colorado, Utah and beyond. Dozens of larger-than-life criminal cowboys are sprinkled through the history of the West, many with names that might be a good handle for a modern boxer or rapper. Rawhide Rawlins, George "Flat Nose" Curry, "Long" Henry Thompson, Charley "Red"

Harvey Logan, aka Kid Curry, appears in John Schwartz's famous "Fort Worth Five" photo of members of the Wild Bunch. Logan is standing at the right, with his hand on the shoulder of Butch Cassidy. Public Domain

Nelson—these were just a few of the notorious thieves and robbers who circulated in northeast Montana, raising hell and sometimes paying for their misdeeds by dancing at the end of a rope.

The most famous of these Montana-based outlaws was probably Harvey Alexander Logan, an Iowa-born cowpuncher better known as "Kid" Curry. Reportedly a hard-working cowboy and expert roper, Curry came to Montana with his three brothers—who also nicked the Curry name from a Texan named George "Flat Nose" Curry—in the early 1890s and found work in the Little Rockies along the western edge of Missouri River Country. It wasn't long before Curry embarked on the outlaw life, after an altercation with Pike Landusky, the owner of a gold mining claim near Rocky Point. Landusky was shot to death in a saloon in his eponymous town, the first of several murders attributed to Kid Curry over a ten-year period.

Not long after slipping out of town to avoid jail time, Curry headed south to Colorado and began riding with a group of bank robbers headed by Tom "Black Jack" Ketchum. After knocking over a bank in Belle Fourche, South Dakota, the gang rode to Montana to continue their crime spree. Eventually, after a disagreement with Ketchum over his cut in a train robbery, Curry and his brother George left the gang and joined up with Butch Cassidy and the Sundance Kid, riding with the Wild Bunch. The crew went on to roam the western territory, eventually becoming the most successful train robbing gang in the country. The Wild Bunch was part of the legendary Hole-in-the-Wall Gang, a loose conglomeration of outlaw bands named for the geologically perfect Hole-in-the-Wall Pass in Wyoming, a notch in the Big Horn Mountains where they maintained a hideout, and lawmen could not approach undetected. At the end of the 1800s the Wild Bunch began to gain notoriety. Their daring heist of a Union Pacific passenger train near Wilcox, Wyoming, on June 2, 1899, was the basis of the popular movie *Butch Cassidy and the Sundance Kid*. Based loosely on fact, the 1969 film was famously headlined by Robert Redford and Paul Newman, but also featured Ted Cassidy (who also played Lurch in TV's *The Addams Family*) as Kid Curry.

After the famous heist in Wilcox, Curry spent a fair amount of his days circling back to Montana, where he would lay low in the Missouri Breaks, eluding capture by the Pinkerton detectives, contracted killers, and various lawmen who sought to make their careers by capturing the man who became known as "the wildest of the Wild Bunch." He spent much of his time on the Logan ranch in Landusky, and some striking evidence of Curry's presence in the area was recently found near Ingomar. "Kid Curry 1901" is carved into a sandstone monolith about five miles north of Highway 12. The carving has been documented and its photograph entered into the Smithsonian Institute collection, and expert handwriting comparisons suggest that this was the actual Kid Curry's handiwork. He was in the area at the time, as he reportedly robbed a Great Northern train at Wagner, in Phillips County, on July 3 of that year. He and his gang got away with an estimated $40,000 worth of unsigned bank notes.

After a decade that saw him credited with seven robberies, nine killings and at least two jailbreaks, Kid Curry's notorious ride through the Wild West would finally come to an end in dramatic fashion that would befit the legend of one of Montana's most notable outlaws. It happened on June 7, 1904, when Curry and two other men robbed a westbound San Francisco Express near Parachute, Colorado, and led a growing posse on a frantic two-day chase across the Colorado River into the plains, where the bandits fueled their escape by stealing horses and provisions from several ranches. A six-man posse eventually cornered the trio on a steep ridge near East Divide Creek. At this point the outlaws, having lost their horses, faced imminent capture or death. A shootout erupted, and Curry was plugged by a rancher named Rolla Gardner, who was crouched behind the body of his horse which had just been shot out from under him by Curry. The slug hit Curry's shoulder, plowed through his rib cage, shattered his sternum, and tore through his other arm. Curry realized that he was at the end of his trail, facing either a slow, painful death or life in prison. For much of his outlaw career, Kid Curry had bragged that he would never be taken alive by a lawman and, true to his word, he put the barrel of his pistol to his temple and pulled the trigger. For his efforts in bringing about the demise of one of America's most wanted men, Gardner received $25 and a new horse.

Kid Curry, though, is the one whose legend lives on, surrounded by the mystique of the Wild West outlaw. The endless expanse of Missouri River Country, with its target-rich railroads and vast geography in which to lay low, proved irresistible to Curry and dozens of other outlaws who left their bloody mark on Western history.

PALLID STURGEON AND THE LOWER YELLOWSTONE IRRIGATION PROJECT

AMONG MONTANA'S LAUDED FISH SPECIES, the sleek and sexy trout get most of the glory, sometimes sharing the spotlight with arctic grayling or warm-water game fish like walleye or bass, but pity the pallid sturgeon, the Ernest Borgnine of Montana's native fish. This pale, duck-billed creature looks like a cross between an alligator and a shark, if maybe somehow there was an armadillo involved. It wears its prehistoric origins on it bony sleeve and can grow as big as 5 feet long and 85 pounds at full maturity, which takes 15 years. Although it can live as long as 100 years, it spawns infrequently and demands a fairly specific environment for its eggs to survive. The pallid sturgeon is a living dinosaur, having changed little since the Cretaceous period 70 million years ago.

Once abundant in the Missouri and Yellowstone Rivers and along the entire Mississippi River drainage, their numbers began to drop as dams appeared along the Missouri in the mid-twentieth century. By the 1990s, their habitat degraded so much that the pallid sturgeon was placed on the endangered species list. By 2005 there were ninety fish left in the upper Missouri drainage, all living in a short stretch of the Yellowstone. An aging population survived in the lower Mississippi River, but natural procreation had all but stopped.

The Yellowstone River is frequently called the longest undammed river in America. That's not true. It has at least seven dams, four of them between Sidney and Billings in its lower stretch. They're not hydroelectric structures, nor are they there for flood control. They're all submerged dams, called weirs, and they're there for one purpose— to divert water from the Yellowstone for irrigation on the surrounding farmland.

The weir between Sidney and Lake Sakakawea in North Dakota, the vast body of water where all the pallid sturgeon eggs used to drift after spawning had taken place far upstream, is now the focus of the Lower Yellowstone Irrigation Project

The original wooden frame structure still stands at the Lower Yellowstone Irrigation Project dam near Sidney.

(LYIP). Although the weir at Sidney is submerged, it's piled shore to shore with huge boulders that protrude above the river's surface, except during the high-water flows of spring. Pallid sturgeon are big, but they are not nearly athletic enough to propel themselves up and over the boulders, salmon-style, to reach their spawning grounds upstream. To save the pallid sturgeon from extinction, several government agencies, along with the State of Montana and the Nature Conservancy, signed an agreement in 2005 to analyze the situation and come up with an alternative plan for the sturgeon to bypass the Intake Diversion Dam.

An Environmental Assessment was completed in 2010. Fish screens were installed. A rock ramp was designed. Head gates were adjusted to produce the proper turbulence

and suction that would not interfere with larval drift or allow eggs to flow into the irrigation canal. Public meetings were held in Glendive, Sidney, and Billings, drawing hundreds of people who wanted to voice their support of the project.

"The Environmental Assessment was two thousand pages long," says James Brower, who'd come onboard as the LYIP manager in 2012. "We planned for twelve fish gates, even though we were told we only needed eleven." After the screens and head gates were put into use, however, the overall plan was deemed unworkable. By 2015 a new plan had emerged, and it was elegantly simple: They would build a bypass channel around the dam.

That's when the lawsuit hit.

In 2015 the Defenders of Wildlife and the Natural Resource Defense Council filed a lawsuit alleging that the LYIP was in violation of the Endangered Species Act. The suit's aim was to remove every diversion dam on the river completely, "restoring the area to its pristine, Lewis and Clark-era condition," says Brower. The stakes were huge, with two things hanging in the balance—the survival of a species that had been around for millions of years, and the ongoing way of life for hundreds of families in Richland County who depend on irrigation. An estimated 2310 jobs would be lost without the diversion and its irrigation. The aquifer would dry up. There would be no drinking water from the wells.

Judge Brian Morris presided over the first of four hearings in Great Falls, where more than twenty people from Sidney had made the six-hour bus trip to voice their concerns. Hundreds filed declarations of support of the fish bypass that would allow the dam to remain. Later that summer the court granted an injunction, halting work on the bypass. Construction equipment was sent back to Denver, says Brower, at a cost of a million dollars. "The reason this case dragged on so long," he adds, "is that it's different than what it sounds like."

The plaintiffs recommended that Sidney should install a series of massive irrigation pumps at a cost of $132 million. Two years later, in 2017, the agencies involved completed a supplemental EIS that concluded that the bypass was, indeed, the best solution. The lawsuit could have ended then, says Brower, had Judge Morris simply gone to the dam at Intake to see for himself what the proposed bypass would look like. Instead, the judge issued yet another injunction, stopping work on the bypass.

Finally, the LYIP won a victory through the Ninth Circuit Court of Appeals. On April 4, 2018, that court issued a negative review of Judge Morris's decisions, and the injunction was lifted. There would be no more appeals from the plaintiffs.

Sidney held a parade at the end of summer to celebrate the salvation of the town's livelihood.

Today, the Yellowstone River flows over the weir at Intake, oblivious to the mighty struggle that took place over the future of its waters. James Brower looks across the river at the bypass, then takes a few minutes to inspect the gleaming chrome drums of the $27 million fish screen. Although the main bypass is not completed, he's not worried about the sturgeon. Some tagged specimens have already made it upstream through the preliminary bypass. "This isn't just us winning," he says about the Sidney farming community's legal victory. "Now it sets legal precedence where other farmers can go back to our case. This is the way we should approach saving these endangered species." After two and a half years spent fighting for his project in courtrooms, he's happy to be able to just do the job he loves. "Water is one of the most powerful forces on earth. That's why I got into irrigation."

MONTANA'S OWN BRIDGE TO NOWHERE

MONTANA HAS SOME GREAT BRIDGES. Snowden Bridge in Nohly isn't the highest—that honor belongs to the Koocanusa Bridge near Eureka, which at 270 feet above Lake Koocanusa, is higher than the Golden Gate Bridge. Nor is Snowden Montana's oldest bridge. In Fort Benton, the five-span steel behemoth that spans the Missouri River holds that title, having been built in 1888, some 25 years before the Snowden Bridge was opened. There are prettier bridges, busier bridges, and longer bridges (also the Koocanusa), but the Snowden Bridge, when completed, had one claim to fame that still stands: it was the longest vertical lift bridge in Montana.

It's still there on the Missouri River, this engineering marvel that connects Roosevelt County to Richland County, just a few miles from the North Dakota border. Based on the South Halsted Street Bridge in Chicago, the structure is 1,159 feet long, and cost $465,367 to build in 1913. Such an undertaking today would run more than ten million dollars. Built by the Montana Eastern Railway along with its twin, the Fairview Bridge, ten miles away over the Missouri River in North Dakota, the bridges would allow the railway to connect New Rockford, N.D. with Lewistown, Montana. However, in one of the biggest cases of irony in Montana's early railroad history, the magnificent design of the Snowden Bridge was instrumental in creating its own demise. Before it welcomed its first train, it was already obsolete.

The Snowden Bridge spans the Missouri River near Nohly.
Photo courtesy of
MonDak Heritage Center

The Yellowstone River originates in the Absaroka Range in northwestern Wyoming, flows north through its namesake lake and national park, picks up several tributaries as it winds northeast through Montana, then dumps its muddy contents into the Missouri River. The area surrounding the confluence, near the town of Williston, North Dakota, is a mother lode of historic significance. Fort Union, constructed by the American Fur Company 25 miles to the west, was the most important trading post in the territory for 40 years. Assiniboine, Lakota, Hidatsa and other Northern Plains tribes traveled to the post to trade peacefully with Canadian and American fur traders. Nearby Fort Buford was established by the U.S. Army in 1861 and was immediately attacked by a band of Hunkpapa Lakota led by Sitting Bull. After years of skirmishes, including the Battle of Little Big Horn, the famed Sioux chief surrendered at the Fort in 1881.

When Montana and North Dakota achieved statehood within a week of each other in 1889, the two states adopted opposing positions on the sale of alcohol. Montana allowed it, North Dakota did not. With railroad and river traffic bringing more people to the confluence area, a border town sprouted in the badlands to serve the thirsty folk of North Dakota. The town of Mondak was established near the confluence in 1903, and soon nearly a dozen saloons lined its main thoroughfare. It quickly earned a reputation as the toughest town in the west, with violence and lynching becoming almost commonplace. The Missouri River's largest ferry served the town, allowing passage over the river between the two states, and the need for a bridge across the river in order to expand the Great Northern Railway through Mondak became apparent. The Snowden Bridge was proposed in 1906, funding was secured, and construction began in 1912.

The bridge would need to accommodate the steamships that navigated the Missouri, which was a major pre-railroad shipping route. The structure was designed to have an entire span lifted by a cable and pulley system, assisted by offset weights. The mechanism was so well-balanced that it was powered by a small, three-cylinder kerosene engine that was housed in a tiny enclosure atop the span. The engine could lift the span 43 feet in 30 minutes, although the system could also be hoisted by a hand crank.

By the time the bridge opened in 1913, however, steamship traffic on the Missouri River was almost nil. The very railroad system that the bridge helped expand was supplanting inland waterborne freight. The moveable, exquisitely balanced steel spans of the Snowden Bridge and its brother in Fairfield were reportedly lifted just once, when they were tested upon completion.

The town of Mondak, the saloons of which had provided so much traffic for the railway and ferry, lost its raison d'être when National Prohibition took effect in 1920. The population quickly dwindled, and a prairie fire in 1927 finished the job, wiping out all but a few buildings, which remain as a ghost town.

Wooden planking was added to the Snowden Bridge in 1925 to allow motor vehicles to share the bridge with trains. Crossing gates were installed to stop traffic when a train was coming, and sometimes vehicles would have to back up off the bridge to avoid a collision. Just to make things a little more interesting, pedestrians were also allowed to use the bridge. As crazy as it sounds, this went on for decades. The 1981 Environmental Impact Statement for the new Mondak motor vehicle bridge stated that the situation was "so dangerous that it [was] safe" because people were extraordinarily careful when crossing the bridge.

The Mondak vehicle bridge, just downstream in North Dakota, opened in 1985, so no cars cross the Snowden Bridge anymore, although it still carries the occasional train. State route 147 can take you there to its spot on the Missouri, where it looms up in the middle of nowhere, a monument to a bygone era of steamships, and an ongoing symbol of architectural ambition cut off at the legs by short-sightedness, trapped on the wrong side of transportation history.

EAST VS. WEST:
A TALE OF TWO STEREOTYPES

Western Montana. That's where all the Marxist hippies live, right? You know, Trustafarian "recreationists" who swath themselves in tie-died Gore-Tex and drive their hybrid cars to the organic market to drink kombucha and plan the next gay pride parade. And how about those Eastern Montanans? Aren't they all raw-boned ranchers with Reagan portraits over their beds, stoic loners who gnaw on a plug of tobacco as they squint into the sunset and curse the leftist lawmakers in Helena who all believe that Montana ends at Billings? Sadly, these cartoonish stereotypes are still common throughout the state. Using a broad brush to paint the residents of such a huge, diverse state is small-minded, divisive, and completely unfair. But, as with most stereotypes, at the center of each of these overblown characterizations lies a little kernel of truth.

Montana's settlement was largely dictated by its geography. While most of the states were settled from east to west, Montana went the other way. The

The Big Sky doesn't get much bigger
than over the Rocky Mountain Front.
Photo © Lyle James Photography

resource-rich western third of Montana originally drew settlers in far greater numbers than those who would eventually carve out their place in the east. Most of those who worked their way past the Great Divide held visions of riches and luxury, courtesy of the abundant natural resources. People came to western Montana in droves during the Gold Rush to make a killing. In eastern Montana, where the riches were the land itself, they came to make a living. The gold rush and mining booms in the Northern Rockies saw settlements spreading through the mountain West beginning in the mid-1800s, but in eastern Montana the only European strongholds during that time were military forts. Miles City, for example, wasn't even established until 1876.

As Montana began to be more fully populated at the turn of the twentieth century, a pattern emerged. The state's monetary resources were disproportionately funneled to the west. Mining companies and logging interests held sway over the state legislature because they held the power of the economy. They had the numbers. They had the population. And the population worked for them. Possibly as a reaction to this, the ranchers and farmers of eastern Montana grew more independent from the rest of the state. They supplied their own produce, dairy, grain, meat—most of the consumables that kept them self-sufficient.

With logging in the west, agriculture in the east, and the railroad system to tie it all together, not much changed in the big picture for a century or so. The population centers west of the Divide continued to grow, and Montana's tourism industry was bolstered by the establishment of Glacier National Park in 1910.

Cultural trends and other influences brought in by visitors and transplants continually affect the socio-economic landscape of the more densely populated areas of western Montana, while the largely rural eastern half of the state seems more immune—or indifferent—to the winds of change. This led some in the west, especially those who've never spent any time out east, to assume that there's not much going on east of Billings.

"'There's nothing out there east of Helena,'" said one Sidney native. "You hear that sort of thing. Well, eastern Montanans aren't dumb. And they're not deaf. They know those things are being said. Well, then you have to wonder, what are they saying about the people in western Montana?" Indeed, a common reaction to many who live and work in Missouri River Country and Custer Country, when asked about their view of western Montana is resentment. They're frustrated at being written off by those who know little or nothing about their part of the state, the part that provides so much in terms of agriculture and natural resources, not to mention taxes derived from energy production.

One of the myths believed by many in eastern Montana, especially those who haven't spent much time traveling around the western part of the state, is that everyone in the mountain region is politically progressive. This generalization couldn't be much further from the truth.

Yes, there is Missoula, poster child for liberal politics, the town that passed its own nuclear-free ordinance in the seventies and contains Montana's biggest LGBTQ community. But it's the outlier in a red state that was carried by the 2016 Republican presidential candidate by more than twenty percentage points. You don't have to venture far from Missoula to leave its liberal bubble. Hamilton, just 46 miles to its south, is a major conservative stronghold. Up north, Kalispell is known as a Republican town. It's Montana's seventh-largest city, and one of its fastest-growing.

Western Montanans can be a little smug. There's plenty to brag about in the west, with its forested peaks, spectacular waterfalls, trout-filled rivers and man-made cultural attractions, but as Montana continues to grow in population, there's less elbow room to be found in the west, and newcomers laden with money are pushing the cost of living in some cities higher than can be afforded by typical Montanans. Back east, where the land flattens out and there are more cows than people, elbow room isn't a problem. People spend their whole lives living in Missouri River Country and Custer Country, and with good reason. There is no shortage of eye candy. The sandstone sculptures of the Missouri Breaks National Monument are every bit as breathtaking as the mountains of Glacier or the rugged vistas of the Bob Marshall Wilderness. Fort Peck Lake is home to some world-class walleye fishing and is surrounded by the C.M. Russell National Wildlife Refuge, teeming with wildlife and full of stunning scenery. When you're looking at the variety of terrain and people in a state as big and as geographically diverse as Montana, you may want to consider that our shared love for Big Sky Country could be the common factor that brings us together more than keeps us apart.

CUSTER
COUNTRY

THE PEOPLE YOU MEET IN CUSTER COUNTRY are in love with the land. Agriculture and ranching dominate the economy, and Billings, Montana's biggest city, is headquarters of the state's energy industry. Talk to a rancher in Ryegate, and he'll tell you all about being a third-generation landowner whose kids will one day take over the ranch. It's the same in Ekalaka, where people born and raised there have no use for faraway places like Whitefish or Great Falls. Many have never been. That's okay with them. They know they're already in the heart of the wide-open spaces, the true Montana that inspires an openness, a generosity of spirit that you encounter everywhere around here.

The Musselshell River occasionally swells well beyond its banks during late spring runoff, as it did here, flooding the city park in Harlowton.

Most campsites at Medicine Rocks State Park are nestled among the giant, carved rocks.

The Yellowstone River is Custer Country's life-blood, running along I-90, Montana's main traffic corridor, from Laurel all the way east to Glendive before it turns north to join with the Missouri. It's a recreational bonanza, offering many great stretches for rafting, as well as fishing for trout and paddlefish.

Custer Country also is home to some of Montana's most interesting blue highways, state routes that thread together dozens of small towns, each with a personality of its own and brimming with historical gems and unique personalities unknown to the world at large. Contrary to the conventional wisdom, outsiders are not shunned here. They're welcomed and treated as friends with whom southeast Montanans can share their deep history and interesting stories. The terrain is strikingly beautiful out here, but it's the people who make it worth spending time getting to know Custer Country. On the Crow Indian Reservation, there's the Little Bighorn Battlefield National Monument, where the region's namesake fought his famous battle with the Sioux and Cheyenne warriors led by Sitting Bull. Originally known as the Custer Battlefield National Monument, the site was renamed in 1991 to better reflect those involved in the battle, which, of course, was General George A. Custer's last.

IN LAUREL, A MEMORIAL FOR ALL MONTANA FIREFIGHTERS

TRENTON JOHNSON PEERED THROUGH the smoke as he hacked away at the undergrowth on Rice Ridge at the edge of the Bob Marshall Wilderness. As he swung the tool in his hand, a Pulaski or perhaps a shovel or a hoe, the 19-year-old may have imagined wielding a lacrosse stick as he did during his four seasons with Hellgate High School's varsity squad in Missoula. The Knights had won the state championship all four years, thanks in part to Trenton's teamwork and aggressiveness as a D-pole, or defender. He was named team captain his senior year. On this Wednesday afternoon in July 2017, however, he had just been deployed with nine other Grayback crew members to try and quell the lightning-started fire just northeast of Seeley Lake. The blaze had covered only half an acre when the crew arrived that day. After an assessment meeting that included identifying escape routes and establishing communications, the Grayback team worked on thinning the fuels on the ground while a helicopter swooped in, dropping buckets of water. This was Trenton's first season as a wildland firefighter. He'd completed the

The Firefighters Memorial in Laurel honors all firefighters in Montana.

40-hour training program and a day of field exercises and had just enjoyed a couple of days off after two weeks spent mopping up a fire in Utah. While more experienced crew members used chainsaws to clear branches along the fire line, the blonde, blue-eyed young man was probably buoying his fellow firefighters with his upbeat chatter, as he was known to do.

The crew was making solid progress against the fire when tragedy struck. "It was as fast as a lightning bolt," Grayback President Michael Wheelock said in an interview with the *Missoulian*. "They just heard a crack and that was it. Three of them were able to get out of the way, and Trenton didn't." A burning snag snapped and crashed down toward a group of firefighters, landing on Johnson. He was airlifted to St. Patrick Hospital in Missoula, where he died soon after, the first firefighter claimed in the 2017 fire season. Two weeks later, another firefighter would be killed by a falling tree while battling the massive Lolo Creek blaze near Missoula.

As of this writing, 42 wildland firefighters have died while fighting Montana wildfires, according to the National Interagency Fire Center. That includes the 13 smokejumpers killed in a single incident, the tragic Mann Gulch fire of 1949. In that situation, 15 smokejumpers parachuted into the Mann Gulch near Helena, but were trapped by the flames from an unexpected change of wind. Two survived. Firefighters like Trenton Johnson, and the men who paid the ultimate price for their dedication at Mann Gulch, along with the others whose courage is their legacy are finally receiving lasting recognition for their valor at the new Montana State Firefighters Memorial in Laurel, which was opened with a dedication ceremony on September 8, 2018. The Memorial pays tribute not just to wildland firefighters, but to fallen firefighters of all types, including city firefighters, volunteer department members, Department of Natural Resources and Conservation employees, tribal fire department members and others who lay their lives on the line every time they go out to battle a blaze.

"It's a park that memorializes the ultimate sacrifice of all firefighters," said Marcia Hafner of the Laurel Chamber of Commerce. The memorial is located in the town's "safety complex," which includes the Police Department, the Laurel Volunteer Fire Department and the Laurel Volunteer Ambulance Department. The landscaped park on the corner of Second Avenue and West Second Street occupies a quarter of the block, and the design provides for a serene setting for reflection on the lives lost by Montana firefighters. A paved circle in the center of the space features polished, black granite slabs etched with the names of 73 Montana firefighters who have died in the line of duty since 1895.

The idea for the monument was introduced in 2004 by Laurel's then-mayor Ken Olson, who was also a firefighter for 22 years. Ground was broken on the site, but the project languished for 13 years due to lack of funding and other issues. When Montana's Legislative session of early 2017 saw a bill introduced that suggested moving the memorial to Helena, Laurel's firefighter community snapped into action. The Laurel Urban Revitalization Association got involved with the project, TIF funds were secured, and half a dozen volunteers worked at implementing the memorial's design, which will cost an estimated $250,000 when all is said and done. This includes dramatic lighting to showcase the monument after dark. The tree-ringed park is a highly detailed oasis in Laurel's downtown area, providing a respectful yet inviting vibe. A concrete path connects a garden of native grasses and daffodils to a large paved circle where the U.S. flag is flanked by the Montana state flag and the official flag of Montana's Firefighters flag that bears the legend, "Loyal to Our Duty." All three flags fly at half-staff in a perpetual show of respect for Montana's fallen firefighters.

The dedication ceremony in September 2018 drew a crowd of several hundred people, including delegations from all three of Montana's congressional representatives. Montana Attorney General Tim Fox spoke of the courage of first responders like those who ran headfirst into the horrific chaos at Ground Zero on 9/11. "I don't think anyone can fully prepare for the circumstances firefighters face while on duty," he said. "They rely on their training and do the job."

Montana's wildfires make national news each summer, and the state's smokejumpers are famous for their courage in the face of overwhelming danger. All firefighters, though, whether urban, volunteer or wildland, put their lives on the line and sometimes pay the ultimate price. Thanks to the perseverance and vision of a handful of firefighters in Laurel, all of Montana is represented at a memorial the firefighting community can call their own. It's a place for reflection, where the courage and sacrifice of people like Trenton Johnson are honored.

HISTORY ON THE WALLS AT PICTOGRAPH STATE PARK

FROM THOMPSON FALLS STATE PARK in the northwest to Medicine Rocks State Park in the southeast, Montana's fifty-five state parks draw hundreds of thousands of visitors each year. Even before the State Parks Commission was created in 1939, people clambered through the Lewis and Clark Caverns, Montana's first state park, designated in 1936. Compared to Pictograph State Park, however, those venerable caverns south of Three Forks still have that new-state-park smell. Evidence shows that people have been visiting the sandstone caves of Pictograph State Park for more than 10,000 years. It's become one of the most important archaeological sites on the Northern Plains, and it's about ten minutes from downtown Billings.

It's a postcard-perfect drive along the winding asphalt to the caves, just off Exit 452 on I-90, five miles from Billings. A compact interpretive center sits near the foot of the towering sandstone cliffs that house a series of three large, bowl-shaped caves, the central attraction of the 23-acre park. The site has yielded more than 70,000 artifacts

Pictograph State Park, one of the most significant cultural native sites in the West, is ten minutes from downtown Billings.

since official archaeological excavations began in 1937. Pictograph Cave, the largest, held 40,000 of them. It's also the cave where the namesake drawings can still be seen on the cave walls. You have to look hard, though—over the years water and vandalism have degraded the images to the point where they're barely visible. Fortunately, detailed interpretive signs show the original images and the positions of the drawings in the cave, and once you know what you're looking for the pictures become more evident. The oldest of the drawings, a turtle, has been radiocarbon dated to 2100 years old. Artifacts such as bone tools, jewelry, and seashells procured from West Coast tribes show that indigenous peoples have been inhabiting the caves for 10,000 years or more. Excavations were halted just after the U.S. entered World War II upon the bombing of Pearl Harbor, and were not resumed. Ongoing research suggests that this dramatic little state park in Custer Country might be the oldest archaeological site in North America. The incredible number of artifacts discovered in just four years of exploration during the original excavations suggest a vast number of manmade items remain in the earth.

Scientists have identified 106 individual paintings and drawings in Pictograph Cave, which were made between 2100 and 200 years ago. The earliest pictures are as high as fifteen feet up the cave wall (excavation removed at least ten feet of material from the cave floor). Most pictures were made by painting red, white or yellow figures over black line drawings. Depictions of all kinds of animals and human figures fill the walls, and even a few rifles were added as recently as the 19th century. While some of the pictures are easily identifiable, many are the subject of debate about their interpretation. Unknown symbols and cryptic images hold clues to the cultures of the early visitors to the caves, but some of those tribal codes may never be cracked. Many tribes are known to have used the caves for shelter over the millennia, and some still treat the area as a mystical site, performing tobacco ceremonies and other native rituals. Modern visitors are strongly discouraged from adding their own artwork—the state has roped off access to the walls containing the fragile images, and warnings of a $750 fine for defacing the site are posted near the caves.

A wide concrete path provides smooth but steep access as it curves gracefully through the trees up a slope to Pictograph, the first of the three caves. It's a favorite hangout of swallows, and hundreds of the birds fill the air in the caves and along the cliffs as they gather insects to feed their young, which are tucked away in the hundreds of dried mud nests clinging to the walls and ceilings. There are a couple of picnic tables tucked in among the vegetation near the base of the trail, providing a nice, shady spot to rest or enjoy some lunch. As you approach Pictograph Cave, you may be overtaken by a feeling of reverence and calm, like you might get upon entering a church. Take a moment to remind yourself that you're treading the same ground once walked by moccasin-clad feet hundreds or thousands of years ago. This is where indigenous peoples came to record their history, to tell the story of their existence or to leave messages to anyone who might enter the caves after they left. This was their social media.

Although there are bolder, more obvious examples of cave art in sites throughout North America, such as the petroglyphs left by the Anasazi in the southwest and prehistoric cave paintings recently discovered in Tennessee's Cumberland Plateau, you'd be hard-pressed to find such an accessible site of ancient indigenous culture so close to a metropolitan area. You can occasionally see jets pass by overhead, landing gear down, on approach to Billings Logan International Airport. Still, it's just far enough off the interstate where the calm ambience of the caves is not disturbed by the rumble of passing tractor-trailers.

Humans are not the only creatures to have frequented the caves. The bones of carnivores and raptors have been found at the site, as well as remains of larger beasts such as bison and elk, suggesting that all manner of species have brought their kills to the caves to consume or process. The caves provide massive natural shelter from sun, wind, rain and snow. The tall, deep cavern at the left end may even provide shelter for some spirits, according to the reports of some visitors. It's called Ghost Cave, and sometimes the swirling winds can create whooshing sounds that seem to emanate from the back of the cave, conjuring images of malevolent spirits. There have also been claims, or perhaps stories handed down through the generations, of the caves being a dwelling place of the Wendigo, a cannibalistic beast of Chippewa legend. There's definitely a mystical energy that permeates the caves, but it's up to the visitor how to interpret that.

Montana residents can visit Pictograph State Park for free. Nonresidents pay a small fee.

THE JERSEY LILLY, JEWEL OF HIGHWAY 12

A FRIEND OF MINE MAKES FREQUENT TRIPS from his home in Missoula to his family ranch in Richland County near the North Dakota border where the Yellowstone River folds into the mighty Missouri. Summer and winter, he tends to drive the state highways, eschewing the bland, efficient interstate in favor of the quirky people and historic hot spots that abound along the two-lane blacktop. He may vary his route a bit, but he always takes Highway 12 between Forsyth and Roundup. He never misses a chance to stop at one of his favorite eateries in Montana. Whenever he speaks of it, his eyes mist over with affection and nostalgia. "Ah," he says, softening his voice as if speaking of a lover who left an indelible mark on his heart. "The Jersey Lil."

He's talking about the Jersey Lilly Bar & Cafe in Ingomar, the sole surviving business in a former railroad stop that was once known as the sheep-shearing capital of the world. At its peak in the early 20th century Ingomar had 600 residents, but now barely a dozen people make their home in this unincorporated area. The Jersey Lilly, though, remains busy, filled with area ranchers and farmers as well as adventurous travelers who are willing, like my friend, to break free of the interstate and see the "real" Montana.

The interior of the Jersey Lilly has remained largely unchanged since its beginnings in 1933.

The long brick building is surrounded by a boardwalk, and the two outhouses are visible off the back corner. When you enter through the heavy wood front door, it's like walking through a time machine into the Old West. The ornate back bar, which was shipped up the Yellowstone and Missouri Rivers from St. Louis in the early 1900s, is replete with intricately carved designs and inlaid with strips of leaded glass. All kinds of decorations and doo-dads are crammed onto the shelves, from stuffed game birds to a jackalope to a sign bearing a picture of a Colt Revolver and the attendant warning, "We Don't Dial 911." Framed photos of cowboys and ranchers and the occasional celebrity adorn every wall of the saloon, and a life-sized cardboard cutout of John Wayne watches the action from one end of the room while a mounted bison head wearing a small top hat gazes down from the other.

The Jersey Lilly started as the Wiley, Clark and Greening Bank in 1914. It had the good fortune to be located next to a vacant lot when a catastrophic fire wiped out a dozen other buildings in 1923. As the only water available was trapped rainwater or what supply was hauled in via railroad from Harlowton or Miles City, there was no way to fight the fire. Ingomar eventually rebuilt, but its boom days were over. When the Great Depression hit most of the town left to find work. In 1933 the bank was converted to a bar by Clyde Easterday, who named it the Oasis. It was Bob Seward who named the bar the Jersey Lilly after he took over in 1948. He named it after Judge Roy Bean's saloon in Langtry, Texas, which in turn had been named after a famous British actress who had been born on the Isle of Jersey. In 1958 Seward sold the bar to his son Bill, and that's when the iconic bar and cafe really began to come into its own. In 1963 it was added to the National Historic Register.

The Jersey Lilly was already the grand old dame of Ingomar, having long been established as the hub of the community. Ranchers would travel long distances through the brutal winter landscape to partake in the big Christmas dinner hosted at the cafe. The Sewards continued Bob's tradition until the mid-1990s when health issues forced Bill to sell the bar. During his long tenure behind the bar, Seward—an ex-boxer whose nose had been broken so many times he had to hold his eyeglasses on his face with a cord secured under his sailor's hat—made hundreds of friends and loved to regale visitors with his wild stories. He also, with his wife, Martha, came up with a bizarre menu item that has endured to this day. Sheepherder hors d'oeuvres, as they're called, were born out of the need for sheepherders (never shepherds, please) to carry nonperishable foods out into the field for long periods of time. A slab of sharp cheddar on a saltine, topped with an onion

The bean soup is a requisite part of the Jersey Lilly experience in Ingomar.

slice and an orange wedge may sound like a culinary train wreck, but it's not as bad as you might think.

The main attraction, though, is the beans. Above the cash register in the old western saloon are three words formed in barbed wire: Jersey Lilly Beans. There's always a big pot of pinto beans simmering on the stove, and when you order the bean soup it is quite a production. The soup is served in a speckled enamel pot on a tray with a soup bowl and a plate of homemade croutons surrounding a large bowl of homemade salsa. The beans live up to the hype. Plump pinto beans are firm, not overcooked. The broth is spicy enough on its own, but not enough to overwhelm the seasoning. Fat chunks of lean, cured pork fill out the soup, and before you know it you've eaten the entire pot of beans that looks like it could have fed a family of four.

June Nygren and Boots Kope, the current owners of the Jersey Lilly, have carried on the traditional atmosphere of the venerated business, while adding some improvements to the menu like top notch steaks and killer burgers. It's still a gathering place for the locals, in a part of the state where "local" could mean a hundred miles away. Montana still has its share of old saloons, but there's only one Jersey Lilly. For more than a century the solid brick structure has held its ground, providing a backbone to a community that hangs on to its deep Montana traditions as if the last century never happened.

FISHING FOR DINOSAURS

JOHNNY CASH RELEASED A NOVELTY SONG in 1976 called "One Piece at a Time." The story about a couple of auto plant workers who assemble a car by smuggling its mismatched components out of the factory over 25 years was a number one hit. If you were to write a similar song, but substituted a fish for a car, you might wind up with something like the paddlefish. Montana's largest native fish looks like it might have been cobbled together from a few different animals. It has the smooth skin and cartilaginous bone structure of a shark, the plankton-filtering system like that of a baleen whale, and a long, paddle-shaped appendage that resembles a beaver tail protruding from its snout. As strange as its appearance might be, this prehistoric relative of the sturgeon has become a highly-prized game fish valued for its roe, which is second only to the sturgeon in supplying caviar to the world market. The American Paddlefish is native to the Missouri and Mississippi Basins. In Montana, however, the paddlefish is found in just two of Montana's rivers, the Yellowstone and Missouri, and since they were designated as a gamefish in 1963, paddlefishing has become a big deal in eastern Montana.

"It's a very powerful fish," said Montana Fisheries biologist Cody Nagel in a recent video taken on the Missouri River. He and a small crew were

A fisherman with a trophy paddlefish.
Photo courtesy Micah DeHenau

netting and tagging the fish as they moved upstream. "Sometimes when the fish are migrating really hard . . . when they hit the net, they hit it with such force they almost come out of the water." The Fish, Wildlife and Parks (FWP) keeps close track of the paddlefish population to help maintain a balance in the fishery. They take a long time to mature; females usually don't spawn until seven to ten years old, and paddlefish can live 30 years or longer. These fish, which have been around for 300 million years, spawn when the water is high and roiling in May and June, and the brevity of the fishing season reflects a delicate balance. Typically, the season lasts just six weeks, and the state will issue only 1,000 tags. If the harvest limit is reached before the planned closing date, FWP ends the season. Snag and release is allowed for the remainder of the season, however, as long as the population is healthy and at sustainable numbers. That's right—snag, not catch. Paddlefish are filter feeders that live on microscopic zooplankton sifted out of the water through a series of fine filaments near the gills. Bait and lures are useless when fishing for them. Their spatula-like rostrum, or paddle—which is one-third the length of their bodies—is riddled with electroreceptors that can sense weak electrical fields, which help them locate concentrations of zooplankton. As their eyes are tiny and poorly developed, these super-sensitive receptors that extend past the head and along the triangular gill covers are their main means of locating food. Unlike sturgeon, which hug the riverbed sucking food off the bottom, paddlefish stick to the water closer to the surface where zooplankton congregate, swimming slowly around with their huge, toothless mouths open wide.

When angling for paddlefish, locating the quarry can be unpredictable, although they do tend to gather in the same stretches of river. They can be found on the Missouri from Fort Peck to Fort Benton, and the rocky segment of the Yellowstone from the Big Horn River to Intake typically has a great concentration of spawning paddlefish, which migrate upstream from Lake Sakakawea in North Dakota. They spawn on gravel bars, many of which would be in very shallow water or even exposed during normal river flows. Factors such as snowmelt and rain affect the river's flow, which provides the signal for the fish to move. The flood-level runoff of 2018 was so strong that the fish were more spread out, harder for fishermen to find. Still, nearly one thousand paddlefish were taken by anglers in only about three weeks of the season, prompting the FWP to shut it down on June 8.

Fishing for these monsters can be a physical endeavor. They're hauled in by people who wade into the muddy, fast-moving river waters with heavy duty surfcasting gear, using 40-pound test line and heavy lead weights to sling large lightbulb-sized hooks out into the current, hoping the hook will attach to a passing spoonbill by chance. Fishermen may go days on end without any action, but if they do tie into one it can take hours to fight it into shore—a typical paddlefish can be three feet long and weigh in at 40-50 pounds. Montana paddlefish can easily top one hundred pounds; the state record is a 142-pounder hooked on the Missouri in 1973.

The season, which runs mid-May through June, attracts thousands of folks into Glendive, 17 miles upstream from the Intake Diversion Dam. The paddlefishing capital of Montana gets into the act in a big way. Campgrounds are packed with fishermen and -women, who share paddlefish recipes and fishing techniques. Bonds are formed. Beers are consumed. Glendive's Chamber of Commerce has also figured out a clever way to help sustain the paddlefish fisheries program, offering free cleaning of your catch in exchange for whatever roe they harvest. The eggs are processed, packaged and marketed as Yellowstone Caviar, the proceeds of which are used to fund fisheries programs in eastern Montana.

Although it's the colorful, photogenic trout that gets its likeness in tourism brochures, there's a bigger challenge out there. For those who long to haul in an open sea-sized fish in this landlocked state, the paddlefish is the 800-pound gorilla of Montana's biggest rivers.

*The sandstone sculptures
at Medicine Rocks State
Park are up to 80 feet tall.*

THE MYSTERIES OF MEDICINE ROCKS

JUST OFF I-94 NEAR GLENDIVE, on the far eastern edge of the state, Makoshika State Park—Montana's largest—sprawls over 11,000 acres. Easy access from the interstate makes it one of the most popular as well. Makoshika gets a lot of (well deserved) glory, but one hundred miles to the south you'll find one of Montana's most startling and dramatic geological wonderlands. Medicine Rocks State Park, 14 miles north of Ekalaka, sees very few visitors from outside the area, as it's on a small state highway, really not on the way to anywhere. The locals, however, frequent the park in droves. Medicine Rocks State Park is one of Custer Country's little-known treasures.

When you pull into the park and wend your way through the campground, it's easy to see why indigenous peoples have considered this a sacred place for hundreds, even thousands of years. Sandstone monoliths, some as tall as 80 feet and 200 feet long, rise up from the prairie across 330 acres of scrub and pine-covered rock ridges. Over millions of years, wind and rain have carved the towering rocks into bizarre and whimsical shapes, forming holes, curves, bridges and caves, like something Dr. Seuss might design if he'd worked in clay. The otherworldly appearance of the biscuit-colored structures gives the park a mystical feel, and the energy is palpable. Out here, where there is no urban racket or traffic hum, you're able to hear the wind whooshing through the holes and gaps in the rocks, creating a kind of eerie music.

Several Indian tribes have frequented the area for hundreds of years, and the discovery of old tepee rings suggests that many stayed for several days, perhaps on their way from the Yellowstone River Valley to the Black Hills of South Dakota. Archaeological evidence has been found that shows humans have been visiting the area much longer than that—as early as 11,000 years ago. The area was also known among the Indians as a great source for medicinal plants, which increased its importance to the Natives. Medicine Rocks was also a popular site for vision quests, known as a place "where the spirits stayed, and the medicine men prayed." It's also likely that another attraction found in the area were fossil seashells that could be fashioned into jewelry or decorations and traded. Some of the tribes known to have frequented the Medicine Rocks area are the Assiniboine Sioux, Northern Cheyenne, Crow, Mandan and Hidatsa. The Crow, in particular, placed serious importance on the rocks they considered holy. They gathered each year at Medicine Rocks and made offerings to the "Little

People," a tribe of small but mystic people who lived among the holes in the rocks. The Sioux had a name for the sacred spot: *Inyan-oka-la-ka*, or "Rock with a Hole in It." Indians weren't the only visitors who were struck by the odd, giant rocks. Theodore Roosevelt rode into the area while on a hunting trip in 1883 and was flabbergasted with the strange beauty of the enormous sandstone structures. In his book *Hunting Trips of a Ranch Man* he describes the bizarre monoliths and their setting: "Altogether it was as fantastically beautiful a place as I have ever seen; it seemed impossible that the hand of man should not have had something to do with its formation."

The rocks are not, of course, man-made. Fortunately, we have science to thank for determining their composition and the timeline of their formation. The sandstone that comprises the rocks was created 61 million years ago, when a massive freshwater river flowed over the Fort Union Formation toward an inland sea in northwest South Dakota. The fine-grained sand was deposited in underwater dunes 50 feet high. They compacted under their own weight into stone as the inland seas eventually receded, and then were covered by a saltwater delta, as evidenced by fossils of marine worm burrows that have been found on top of the rocks. After that the elements took over as wind and rain carved the rocks into the crazy shapes we see today.

Something else you can still see on the rocks are hundreds of petroglyphs, scratched into the soft sandstone by early Indian visitors, then later by the settlers who moved into the area and by cowboys who were driving cattle and stopped to carve their names and dates into the rocks. Such vandalism of the rocks is now illegal.

During the first part of the twentieth century, the rocks were on land that was privately owned. In the 1930s Carter County took over ownership of the area, and in 1957 donated the land to the state of Montana. The state highway department, which managed the land, graveled the roads and installed picnic tables and fire rings. In 1965 the area was designated a natural reserve and the state parks division took over. For a short time in the 1990s, the state Fish, Wildlife and Parks division charged a $3 entrance fee to help offset the $20,000 yearly cost to maintain the park. This caused an uproar from the area residents who frequented the park, and within two years the FWP found a solution by designated Medicine Rocks State Park one of 15 "primitive" state parks, meaning there would be vault toilets but no trash pickup; people would have to pack out whatever garbage they generated. This allowed the FWP to do away with the entrance fee. There is a nominal fee for non-residents to camp in one of the 12 campsites, but Montana residents camp for free. There is a pump that provides fresh water near the park entrance.

At Medicine Rocks State Park, the rock formations take on otherworldly shapes.

It's a smallish campground, but Medicine Rocks' remote location pretty much guarantees you'll have a few sites to choose from. A variety of wildlife roams the area, and you can see pronghorn, mule deer, sharp-tailed grouse, and a dozen species of grassland songbirds. It's also a popular hangout for small flocks of Merriam's wild turkeys, which can frequently be seen strutting among the rocks in the campground, pecking for insects and chattering to one another.

Medicine Rocks State Park provides a singular experience for those who are willing to take a detour from the beaten path. You can watch the drama of a summer thunderstorm marching across the vast prairie, and in the distance long ridges of sandstone resemble trains running along the horizon. Photographers will find plenty of subject matter, and during the "golden hour" just after sunrise or before sunset, the giant rocks seem to take on soft glow as the holes and caves appear more prominent with their lengthening shadows. It's a powerful place, a little corner of Custer Country where you can escape the crowds to listen to the music of the rocks and feel the pull they have had on those who have been drawn here for thousands of years.

*Ed Buchholz displays
his handcrafted wooden
bowls at Colstrip Days.*

A MONTANA COAL TOWN FADES AWAY

IN MANY WAYS, COLSTRIP IS A SUCCESS STORY. It's one of Montana's last company towns, and its 2,300 residents enjoy an average household income of $80,000 per year, twice that of the rest of the state. Their schools are well-funded. A network of groomed trails has been built through the area, and residents enjoy free golf and free admission to a very nice pool in the city park, complete with a serious water slide. The crime rate is among the lowest in Montana. Most of Colstrip's workforce is employed either by the Rosebud coal mine or by the power plant that burns its coal to produce electricity. Like most of Montana's small towns, it's a close-knit community. Everybody knows everybody else, and its isolated location, 20 miles north of the Northern Cheyenne reservation, only adds to the feeling of unity. For most of its existence, Colstrip seemed to be holding all the cards. Now they're fighting for a spot at the table.

Colstrip was established in 1924 as a Northern Pacific railroad stop where coal could be obtained for their steam-powered locomotives. When the railroad switched from coal to diesel engines in 1958, the Montana Power Company bought the rights to the town and the mine, and in the mid-70s power plants 1 and 2 went online. Ten years later, two more power plants fired up. Colstrip incorporated in 1998, the same year the four power plants were sold to Puget Sound Energy and PPL Corporation of Pennsylvania. The mine also changed hands that year, purchased by Westmoreland Mining LLC.

The power plants use steam to generate electricity, which is transmitted via a massive system of power lines. Not all four plants are operating all the time, occasionally shutting down when there's a glut of power on the grid, as in the spring when rivers are high and hydroelectricity is going strong. When they're all up and running, though, they can produce a staggering 2100 megawatts. Of course, there's a downside. The 700-foot high stacks—the tallest man-made structures in Montana—release CO_2, along with mercury and unhealthy, fine-particulate pollutants. Carbon dioxide is one of the greenhouse gases that contribute to global warming, and the fine-particulate pollutants also contain heavy metals, sulfur dioxide and nitrogen oxides. In 2011 Environment America, using EPA data, ranked the Colstrip plant as the worst offender among the Western states for mercury pollution. Toxic ash has contaminated Colstrip's groundwater enough to render it undrinkable, requiring the town to get its drinking

water from the Yellowstone River, the same source that feeds the power plants. Residents of Colstrip sued the power plant owners in 2008 over the decades of groundwater contamination, which had been caused by leaking coal ash ponds.

The largest coal plant west of the Mississippi, Colstrip's generators have been one of Montana's biggest polluters, dumping an estimated five million tons of carbon pollution into the air every year.

In 2013 the Sierra Club and Montana Environmental Information Center filed a lawsuit against the plant's owners to force them to install up-to-date pollution controls on the aging facilities. A pall of impending doom hung over the town for several years, and the people of Colstrip, who have built their lives and livelihoods around the coal mine and the power plants, have largely been left out of the conversation.

Ed Buchholz is a burly, middle-aged guy with a bushy beard and a broad smile. He's a shift boss at the mine, but on this warm Saturday in July he's in the city park, camouflage ball cap pushed back on his head, standing behind a row of folding tables set up to display his handmade wooden bowls. It's Colstrip Days, and the park is full of people, many stopping by to check out his bowls, which he crafts in his woodshop at home. "My wife says it keeps me out of the house and out of trouble," he says with a chuckle.

Like most everyone who works at the plant and mine, Buchholz feels like Colstrip is getting a bad rap, as he offers his own version of the facts. "The Hawaii volcanoes and (Montana) forest fires put out more gases than these plants ever did," he says. "They have scrubbers and do everything they can to keep emissions in check. The power plant will bend over backward to make sure what's coming out of those stacks is clean as it can possibly be. Everybody works their butt off to make sure everything is right."

The scrubbers Buchholz speaks of do indeed remove up to 95 percent of the CO_2 emissions from the stacks. But, according to a 2017 study by Montana's Bureau of Business and Economic Research, Colstrip still pours three times as much CO_2 into the atmosphere as forest fires in a typical fire season. Still, Colstrip isn't going down without a fight.

Chris Oswald, an AutoCAD engineer who designs reclamation landscapes for the mine, says solar- and wind-generated power aren't reliable. "You can't store electricity. Coal and natural gas can be produced to match the fluctuation in need. The coal plant can go online in ten minutes."

Mayor Duane Ankney, who previously served in the state legislature, is going to the mat for Colstrip. In 2016, before the lawsuit settlement, he told an auditorium full of anxious Colstrip residents, "None of these groups, none of them, are a friend of the working man and woman. They are your enemy. They'll take your job and they'll take the food off your table." To great applause from the crowd, he added, "One positive would be to get Washington (state) the hell out of Montana."

Colstrip native Lori Shaw, 25, also rejects the idea that coal workers must make the transition to renewable energy. She's working the front lines in the so-called "war on coal," running Colstrip United social media accounts to garner community support, and to combat what she calls "lies and ignorance" surrounding the situation. In 2017 the Sierra Club held a "Beyond Coal" meeting in Missoula to discuss, among other issues, the future of Colstrip. No one from Colstrip was invited to attend. Shaw pulled no punches in her response. "Make no mistake about it," she posted on her website, "The citizens of Colstrip and the people of Montana will not simply roll over and resign themselves to being the latest victims of the Sierra Club's short-sighted agenda. They will continue to speak out against the Beyond Coal campaign's assault on the Montana economy and the good paying, high wage jobs that Montana's coal industry provides."

The Sierra Club's lawsuit was settled in 2017, and it signaled the beginning of the end for Colstrip. Rather than pour countless millions into compliance efforts on the aging plants, owner Talen Montana agreed to shut them down entirely. The plant's two older generators would go offline by 2020, and the debt on the newer pair will be paid off by 2027. Part of the lawsuit agreement is a $10 million "community transition fund" that would supposedly help fund the shift from coal power to renewables like solar and wind. While the plants will be mothballed, the transmission lines will be used to continue to send electricity across the state. The plan is for workers to be retrained for jobs in the emerging renewables technologies. For the most part, though, the people of Colstrip aren't buying it.

Their futures are being decided by a consortium of companies that now own the power plants, and they are mostly being left out of the discussion. These are regular people with normal lives, kids in school, mortgages to pay, just like most of us across Montana. As coal prices continue to drop, though, and the evidence of the harmful effects of both its extraction and its use continue to mount, it would seem that the continued use of coal is unlikely in the long term, especially as Montanans increase their use of cheaper natural gas and the developing renewable alternatives like wind and solar. Hopefully, as coal fades away as a viable energy source, the people of Colstrip will be included in the conversation about where we go from here.

Sandstone and limestone
cliffs create rimrock along
Highway 12 near Rygate.

LUMBERING DOWN MONTANA'S DINOSAUR TRAIL

While the bulk of Montana's population is found west of the Continental Divide, there's one group of historical inhabitants that seemed to prefer the broad, open landscapes of central and eastern Montana. At least that's what the bones they left behind would suggest. The bones in question are fossilized. They were dinosaurs, and Montana was lousy with them.

The Dinosaur Trail, a group of 14 museums, sites and interpretive centers that stretches from the Two Medicine Dinosaur Center in Bynum, just east of the Northern Front, to the Carter County Museum in the southeast corner of the state, offers an impressive collection of Montana paleontology. Situated near the Judith River Formation, Hell Creek Formation, Willow Creek Anticline and other paleontological hot spots, these museums have on display some of the most impressive and meaningful fossils ever found in North America, and displays are continually updated as new finds emerge from Montana's fossil-rich landscape. Reconstructed dinosaurs with nicknames like Elvis, Ava, Margie and Big Al are helping scientists piece together the puzzle of life in Montana, some of which dates back to precambrian time.

At the end of the precambrian era—the first 4.5 billion years of Earth's existence—Montana was covered with a shallow inland sea that was home to arthropods, algae, fungi and worms, as evidenced in fossilized specimens that have been found in Glacier Park and other sites throughout the state. As the sea began to recede toward the end of the Cetaceous period, 75 to 80 million years ago, a riparian, subtropical environment provided the perfect habitat for the appearance of several dinosaur species. Choteau and nearby Bynum, northeast of Great Falls in Russell Country, both feature museums full of specimens from the Two Medicine Formation, which was deposited along the western shore of the Late Cretaceous Interior Seaway. Its sandstone rivers and deltas have produced such notable fossils as skulls from the Malasaurus

and the Einosaurus, which are displayed in Choteau's Old Trail Museum in a lifelike mural of their natural environment painted by local artist Jim Utsler. Bynum's Two Medicine Dinosaur Center, besides housing the world's longest dinosaur skeleton, is a more hands-on facility, offering paleontology workshops and a summer "dino-camp" for kids.

To the northeast, up toward the Hi-Line on Highway 2, the Judith River Formation, named for its proximity to the confluence of the Judith and Missouri Rivers, has produced a great number of fossilized remains of creatures from frogs, lizards and fish to large, horned dinosaurs like Judiceratops and Avaceratops. Blaine County Museum in Chinook can be a great place to pick up the Trail, as its displays feature giant marine reptiles like the mosasaur and plesiosaur, as well as reconstructed ankylosaurs, hadrosaurs and other large land animals found in the area.

The Judith River Formation is also home to Egg Mountain, the site of an extremely important fossilized find, one that helped famed paleontologist Jack Horner shore up his theories of dinosaur behavior. Baby dinosaur bones and fossilized eggs showed that some dinosaurs actually raised their young in nurseries, and may have lived in herds throughout their life stages. Horner is Montana's most celebrated dinosaur hunter—more on him in a minute.

Jurassic-era dinosaur fossils are also scattered throughout the state. Northeast of the Egg Mountain area the trail picks up on the Hi-Line with the Depot Museum in Rudyard. The town of about 500 people (and one sorehead, they claim) elects a new "old sorehead" every year, and that title is shared by the "Oldest Sorehead," the museum's fully-articulated Gryposaurus skeleton that was found not far from here.

As the Dinosaur Trail moves eastward into Missouri River Country, Malta's Great Plains Dinosaur Museum and Field Station features a hefty collection of dinosaurs from the Jurassic and Cretaceous periods. A horned species known as Maltaceratops, found in the area, is featured alongside a species of raptor so new it hasn't been named yet. Their most well-known display does have a name, and it is "Leonardo," a duck-billed Brachylophosaurus that was found with sections of soft tissue still preserved, or "mummified." Scientists studying these samples of skin, scales and muscle—even the contents of the animal's stomach—have been able to construct a clearer picture of how the living species may have appeared.

The Badlands is home to the Hell Creek Formation, another productive deposit that has given up some important fossil finds. Makoshika State Park alone has produced at least ten species of dinosaur, including the Edmontosaurus, a complete Triceratops horridus skull, and a *Tyrannosaurus rex*, one of several found in Montana. Makoshika also boasts a nearly complete skeleton of the rare Thescelosaurus, one of the last pre-extinction dinosaurs. As wind, rain and ice continue to work on the sandstone of this fossil-heavy area, new specimens continue to emerge.

The southeast cornerstone of the Dinosaur Trail is Ekalaka's Carter County Museum. Montana's first county museum, it was also the first to display a dinosaur bone found within the state. The museum's Lambert Room boasts an impressive collection, making this a worthwhile out-of-the-way drive for true dinosaur buffs. Their most famous resident is a giant hadrosaur, a duck-billed species of which only five have been found in the U.S. Two of them were unearthed only 30 miles from here. The museum also features the most complete juvenile *T. rex* skeleton found in Montana, as well as the only known specimen of the pterosaur found in the Hell Creek Formation.

The southwest corner of the Dinosaur Trail is the Museum of the Rockies (MOR), in Bozeman.

As a Smithsonian Affiliate, the MOR is recognized as one of the finest research and history museums in the world. It was here that Jack Horner spent 34 years building the facility into a world-class dinosaur study center. The Shelby native also served as technical science advisor for the Jurassic Park movies, and he has helped raise millions of dollars to fund the MOR and its programs. The museum boasts the world's biggest collection of *T. rex* fossils, and has a complete Tyrannosaurus skeleton alongside a full re-creation of an allosaur known as "Big Al." Far from just a collection of bones, the Museum of the Rockies is a multi-dimensional resource with ever-changing exhibits centered on everything from regional history to the evolution of the guitar.

Big Sky Country is big enough to hold mountains of secret history, and many treasures are still out there, buried deep in the ground, waiting for the chance to tell their story. A tour of Montana's Dinosaur Trail can help illustrate that story—through fossils, cultural artifacts and the earth's own footprints that have been revealed—and can also provide some hints about what might turn up in the future.

YELLOWSTONE COUNTRY

THIS CHUNK OF SOUTH-CENTRAL MONTANA that wraps around the northwest corner of Wyoming is a great jumping off point, not only for the original National Park, but for all points in Montana. Yet Yellowstone Country has plenty to give this region its own flavor.

The mountains begin to give way to farmland east of Bozeman.

Just east of the Continental Divide, this is where the Northern Rockies make a last upward surge before the terrain flattens out to the east. For that reason, it's a big-time ski destination. Bridger Bowl, one of Montana's favorite ski areas, is also one of the most challenging—42 percent of its 2,000 acres are double black diamond runs. Down the Gallatin Valley, Big Sky Resort and nearby Moonlight Basin are two of the toniest resorts in Montana. Bozeman, the nearest big town to these ski destinations, is a major hub for several reasons, one of them being Montana State University. It adds a youthful energy to the town's Western vibe, and there's always something happening. On the eastern edge of the region, Red Lodge is more on the blue-collar side, a historic mining town with charm to burn. Stop in for breakfast at Prindy's Place and they'll be happy to tell you about the history of the Beartooth Highway.

If they're not talking about skiing in Yellowstone Country, they're talking about fishing. The fly-fishing culture is deeply embedded in towns like Livingston, which sits at the north end of the Paradise Valley. Livingston is teeming with fly fishing shops and guide services, and the people here take their nightlife seriously. Jimmy Buffett's song "Livingston Saturday Night" was written in 1978, but most of it still rings true, especially at places like the Murray Hotel, where you can dance to some of the best bands in the Northwest, and a local like Jeff Bridges or John Mayer might stop in to check out the tunes.

Of course, it's called Yellowstone Country for a reason, and three out of the park's five gateway communities are here, each with a funky charm of its own. West Yellowstone is bustling year-round—full of snowmobilers in the winter and geyser gazers in the summer. It features a killer historical museum and tons of restaurants and hotels to fit most budgets. The locals just call it "West." Gardiner, to the north, is also a great place to headquarter when making incursions into Yellowstone. The road between Gardiner and the adorable gateway town of Cooke City just outside the remote northeast corner of the park is open year-round, typically the only road you can drive within the park in the dead of winter.

The aforementioned Paradise Valley, where the Yellowstone River runs between Gardiner and Livingston, is one of the prettiest drives in Montana, winter or summer. The Old Saloon in Emigrant, about midway up the valley, appears largely as it did when it was built in 1902. The locals are friendly, and happy to chat with a visitor at the bar. Chico Hot Springs, in Pray, is a favorite haunt of many Montanans, and features some world class dining to boot.

There's a lot to see and do around here, a little something for everybody. Yellowstone Park is grand, but, hey, Yellowstone Country is no slouch.

A NEW KIND OF
MONTANA RANCH

ON THE VALLEY FLOOR JUST WEST OF THE BRIDGER MOUNTAIN RANGE, about 90 miles north of Yellowstone National Park, James and Kathy Rolin are raising the largest herd of farmed animals in Montana. Somewhere between 500,000 and 1,000,000 head are roaming the habitat within the borders of their compound, and the couple wrangles this herd largely on their own. It sounds like an impossible feat until you learn that the animals they're raising average about a half inch in size. Located in a business park near the Belgrade airport, Cowboy Cricket Farms is Montana's first and only cricket ranch, where one answer to the world's food security problem has six legs.

Crickets as food? Welcome to the world of entomophagy, the practice of eating bugs. It's not a new phenomenon, as cultures around the world have been including insects in their diet for hundreds of years. From wax moth larvae to witchetty grubs to grasshoppers, insects provide a terrific source of protein, iron and other nutrients without the environmental havoc wreaked by raising traditional livestock like cattle, pigs, and chickens. According to an exhaustive report released by the Food and Agriculture Organization of the United Nations in 2013, there are currently 1900 species of insects being consumed by people, and many of these bugs can be efficiently farmed to produce a sustainable and healthy source of protein.

Kathy Rolin got the idea for Cowboy Cricket Farms while studying nutrition at MSU under Florence Dunkel, an entomologist and founder of the "bug buffet" she's put on for 30 years with the help of the school's culinary arts program. Kathy and James—they met while both were serving in the Coast Guard—secured the Belgrade facility, found a supplier for breeder crickets, and ramped up their business with promises for contracts with food suppliers from Canada to Mexico to buy their products, which include a protein-rich flour substitute made from powdered crickets. Cowboy Cricket Farms opened in the spring of 2017, and so far, it's kept the couple hopping.

The environmental benefits of insects over traditional livestock weighed heavily in the Rolins' decision to pursue a life of cricket husbandry. Raising traditional livestock uses a mind-boggling amount of the earth's water and arable land. For instance, a kilogram of feedlot beef requires an average of 686 gallons of water to produce. A

Crickets, like these slow-cooked specimens, are loaded with protein and nutrients and are far less taxing on the environment to farm than traditional livestock.

kilogram of crickets can be raised on discarded produce and no additional water, and they are 12 times as efficient as cattle in converting feed to protein. "The more we got into it the more it just made sense," says James. "Not just from a business standpoint but environmental and social standpoint as well." With the earth's human population set to hit nine billion by 2050, we'll be struggling to keep up with the demand for meat. Already, some one billion people suffer from food insecurity worldwide. It's been estimated that as much as eighty percent of the world is already using insects to supplement their diet. The US just needs to get beyond the "ick factor." To that end, James and Kathy spend a lot of their time educating groups about the many benefits of entomophagy, and even provide a tasty example with their Chocolate Chirp cookies, which they bake themselves in a commercial kitchen on the ground floor of the 1160 square foot facility. Aside from the cookies and protein powder, Cowboy Cricket Farms also offers packages of whole roasted crickets. It may seem like a "Fear Factor"-style novelty, but that's because our culture hasn't caught up with the rest of the world when it comes to snacking on bugs. In Mexico, for example, paper cones of roasted grasshoppers are sold at sporting events, gobbled up by *futbol* fans like so much popcorn.

The crickets are prepared without seasoning, but they have a pleasant flavor of their own, kind of nutty and slightly crunchy, like a roasted sunflower seed. When grasshoppers and crickets are cooked at a high temperature, they cook quickly but when eaten tend to dissolve into powder. Kathy reveals that, like a good rack of ribs, the Cowboy Crickets specimens are cooked "low and slow" to preserve the delicate flavor and give the snack bugs a more robust texture. In their immaculate kitchen the crickets come out fresh and flavorful.

Upstairs is the hatchery, which takes up about a third of the building's space. Stacked on rows of industrial shelving in the dim, stifling room are as many as 150 plastic tubs, each providing a habitat for about 5,000 crickets. The juvenile crickets, or "pinheads," mature into harvest-ready adults in about four months. The humid, ninety-degree atmosphere helps them grow at an optimal rate as they crawl around on paper egg cartons and drink from a rag protruding from a water-filled beer bottle, Molotov cocktail-style. The egg cartons are speckled with their waste, which is also collected and sold as "frass," a high-quality fertilizer. James notes with a chuckle that their biggest frass customers by far are farmers who grow medical marijuana.

In their first year of existence, thanks to tireless promotion and a clear enthusiasm for their mission, James and Kathy received more than $100,000 in grants and a handful of awards for their visionary business. In fact, the efforts to propagate the cricket farm model have overshadowed the food-production end of things. They raise about a ton of crickets each year, but most of these are used as breeding stock to supply their growing network of partner farms. They buy the harvested crickets back from the farms and process them in their own facility. They offer day-long and week-long training classes, and with half a dozen farms up and running and more on the way, their efforts are paying off. Cricket farming is gaining a foothold.

"We thought it was going to be a lot more difficult than it has been," said James. Once people get past the idea of eating bugs, he added, they really like the flavor, especially the cookies, which are one of their biggest marketing tools. "As soon as they try it, they just dig right in."

WEST YELLOWSTONE'S SNOWMOBILE TRUCE

YELLOWSTONE IN WINTER—it's a white-blanketed wonderland with dazzling geyser eruptions that freeze in midair, creating the appearance of a shower of diamonds raining down. Shaggy bison swing their enormous heads back and forth through the snow, exposing the grasses that sustain them. Elegant trumpeter swans drift around on geothermal ponds, and raptors perch on tall snags, eyeing the snow for white-on-white prey such as weasels and snowshoe hares. With most of the roads closed, and the occasional snow coach producing the only motorized traffic, Yellowstone in winter is also home to another elusive feature: quiet. Without the summertime throngs of chattering tourists and screaming kids riding around in their diesel-powered motorhomes, or the strings of Harley Davidsons grumbling their way through the park, the delicate sounds of Yellowstone are more evident. The soft hiss of snow tumbling from the laden branches of a lodgepole pine, the grunts and snorts of bison, the bubble and hiss of a geothermal feature across a plain—these are the sounds of winter.

That sonic bliss has a clear enemy, though, and they've been waging battle for decades. For a certain community of outdoor recreationists, winter in Yellowstone means snowmobiling, and snowmobiling means West Yellowstone, which has been called the snowmobiling capital of the world. The park's hundreds of miles of snowmobile trails and snow-covered roads have provided endless possibilities for touring the park aboard a snowmobile since the machines came into vogue in the early sixties. At its peak of popularity, some 80,000 snowmobilers were entering park each winter.

By the late nineties, however, the negative impact of snowmobiles had become apparent. The whine of their two-stroke engines could be heard all over the park. Wildlife was being harassed or chased off the roads, and the hundreds of snowmobilers that lined up at West Yellowstone's park entrance each morning threw so much carbon monoxide and particulate into the air that a gray-blue haze of smoke hung over the town for much of the winter. Park rangers actually took to wearing respirators while stationed at the entrance gates.

Snowmobiles are allowed in Yellowstone Park, but usually as part of a professionally guided group.
Photo courtesy of 123rf.com © delcreations

In 2000, the federal government stepped in, announcing plans to ban snowmobiles entirely from Yellowstone Park. Montana and Wyoming officials protested, saying that the ban would stall the economic engine that kept the park's gateway communities going in the winter. Yellowstone rangers like Rick Bennett, however, felt the ban was imperative for the health of the park's ecosystem. "This place needs to be protected whatever it takes," he said.

The mere announcement of the impending ban caused visitation numbers to plummet, but in his first day in office, President George H. W. Bush announced a moratorium on the ban. Instead, a limit of 720 snowmobilers would be allowed in the park each day, though all snowmobilers would have to be part of a commercially guided tour. A generous limit was also set on snow coaches, the venerable tracked buses that had been doing a booming business since the mid-twentieth century. Throughout the next decade, fewer than 20,000 snowmobilers visited the park each year, while environmental groups, the National Park Service and snowmobile industry factions continued to grapple over the machines' use in Yellowstone. More than half a million public comments have been submitted to the NPS over the controversy, more than any other issue in its entire history, and more than 90% of those comments supported the outright ban of snowmobiles in the park. People feel strongly about Yellowstone and how we should be allowed to enjoy it.

"This is on some level a philosophical—or a symbolic—argument," said Abigail Dillen, an attorney with the Greater Yellowstone Coalition, an alliance of environmental groups. "Yellowstone was the first national park, which makes it iconic and emotionally powerful for Americans."

Businesses in and around Yellowstone Park are, predictably, against any ban. Nonresident snowmobilers who enter the park through West Yellowstone pump an average of $150 a day into the local economy. It's the same in nearby Grand Teton National Park, which is also affected by the snowmobile rules. Wyoming governor Dave Freudenthal echoes the sentiments of many who make their living from visiting snowmobilers. "The people that are suffering under the move toward banning snowmobiles are the small-business owners in and around the parks."

Dillen takes a broader view. "Environmental groups, for their part, believe that Yellowstone belongs to the public and the nation as a whole, not to the snowmobile industry and not to a few local business owners."

Finally, in 2013, a compromise was reached. A big part of the responsibility was placed on the shoulders of the snowmobile manufacturing industry, as the sleds would now be required to be cleaner and quieter. Previously, pollution levels of a snowmobile were ten times that of a car, and new emissions targets were set by the government. To combat noise pollution, a maximum level of 67 decibels, roughly the volume of an average vacuum cleaner, would be required. One avenue to reaching these goals is to use four-stroke rather than the louder, dirtier two-stroke engines. Although the four-strokes are more expensive and deliver less torque, the move has been embraced by the industry.

"This is the most reasonable, the most balanced plan that has ever been presented," said Clyde Seely, a snowmobile operator in West Yellowstone.

As for the park's watchdog groups, they're on board. Tim Stevens of the National Parks Conservation Association feels it's a good solution for Yellowstone. "Absolutely, under this plan Yellowstone will be a cleaner and quieter place, and a place [where] park visitors can find the solitude that is unique to Yellowstone."

Today, the truce seems to be working for those on both sides of the issue. Thanks to the drastically reduced noise and improved air quality, skiers have been returning to the park, adding their dollars to West Yellowstone's economy. Snow coaches carry roughly the same number of visitors into the park as snowmobiles, where they fill rooms at Old Faithful and Mammoth, the park's winter lodges, and keep the Yellowstone's year-round restaurants humming.

As of 2014, the Non-Commercially Guided Snowmobile Access Program allows one group of up to five snowmobilers per day to enter the park at four of its five entrances, without having to hire a commercial guide. As always, snowmobiles must stick to the park's roads and trails, but it's still possible for thousands of people per year to access the park via snowmobile and enjoy the same winter wonderland as skiers, snow-shoers and snowcoach tourists.

UP, UP AND AWAY ON THE BEARTOOTH HIGHWAY

FOR 68 AWE-INSPIRING, JAW-DROPPING, eye-popping miles, State Route 212 between Cooke City and Red Lodge twists up and over Beartooth Pass to create one of the most spectacular drives in the West. Officially, it's the Beartooth National Scenic Byways All-American Road. In Montana, we just call it the Beartooth Highway.

At 10,947 feet, it's the highest highway in the Northern Rockies. Adverse conditions and deep snow close the pass through the winter, but usually by Memorial Day weekend plows are able to cut a channel through the snow, which can be as deep as 26 feet in drifts. Driving along the bottom of a deep slot cut in the snow may not appeal to the claustrophobic traveler, so traffic is pretty sparse until late June or early July, when the snow has melted away from the lower elevations. There's usually snow on the ground at the peak of the pass year-round, and downhill skiing in cutoffs and a t-shirt is a bizarre thrill for many. Once the road is clear and dry in the summer, the Beartooth Highway attracts not just skiers but sight-seers, hikers, photographers and adventurers to its serpentine

Mountain goats, like this juvenile, are a common sight at the peak of the Beartooth Highway.

path through some of the most rugged territory in the Northwest. The byway, which begins and ends in Montana but dips into Wyoming for 35 miles, is surrounded by twenty mountain peaks of more than 12,000 feet. The diversity of terrain, from steep, jagged glaciers to waterfalls to alpine mountain lakes and a broad open plateau, is impressive. More than a million acres of wilderness surround the Beartooth, and wildlife, from marmots to moose, is plentiful. It's also a magnet for motorcycles and low-slung sports cars until the snow flies again in the fall. As many as 1,200 vehicles per day traverse the Beartooth during the summer months, providing an economic boost to Red Lodge and Cooke City. Travel sites suggest planning on two hours to complete the drive, but realistically, that's just for people who are in a hurry to get to the hotel. For the adventurous, the curious, and just those who like to take their time and appreciate its endless natural beauty, the Beartooth can be an excellent all-day meander.

The highway's path might seem random in places, but it has been used for hundreds of years by indigenous peoples and, later, by white hunters and trappers, and the odd Army regiment. After making an inspection tour of the newly designated Yellowstone National Park in 1872, General Philip Sheridan and his 120-man contingent were faced with following the Yellowstone River downstream to Billings from Fort Yellowstone at Mammoth Hot Springs, a long, arduous trek of almost 200 miles. Acting on information from an old hunter named Shuki Greer, Sheridan and his men decided to shave a few miles off their trip by heading east to work their way across the Beartooth Pass. The highway that exists today follows virtually the same route they took.

Opened to auto traffic in 1936, the Beartooth was used largely to transport coal from Cooke City to Red Lodge, which had been a bustling mining town with as many as 6,000 people prior to the Great Depression. The highway was constructed in just five years, providing good wages to hundreds of workers during the Depression. Two men were killed during the construction, which involved dynamiting sections of the rock mountainside to dig out a 15-foot-wide grade. Compared to the efficient and high-tech construction methods of today, the Beartooth could almost be considered an artisanal highway. Much of the work was done with men wielding hand tools such as shovels and picks.

The Beartooth Highway is maintained by Montana but promoted by both states that host its curves. It affords panoramic views of the Beartooth and Absaroka Mountains as it winds between alpine lakes and, in the summer, vast fields of colorful wildflowers bloom among massive glacial boulders. As you travel across the broad peak of the pass, chances are good that you'll see several mountain goats, sometimes right in the road. The horned, white-coated critters are not that shy and have become accustomed to picking up tidbits dropped by sloppy tourists, although intentionally feeding them is illegal. As it drops down the northeast side of the slopes, the road compresses into tight, sidewinder turns as it continues toward the Rock Creek Valley. About two thousand feet below the peak, the Rock Creek Scenic Overlook juts out from the mountainside, providing breathtaking views of Rock Creek Canyon and the Hell Roaring Plateau straight across the valley.

As fun as the suspension-torturing turns of the highway are, this rest stop is worth a look for several reasons. From here, Red Lodge is maybe another 30-minute ride, so it's usually a good time for a bathroom break, and there are plenty of clean restrooms to handle the packs of bikers and kid-stuffed minivans just coming down from the top. A low wall of squared boulders, National Park-style, rim the edge of the overlook, and a paved foot path with sturdy metal handrails extends for about fifty yards out along the spine of an outcrop, ending at a 15-foot-wide circle with a 360-degree view. From the path it appears to be a sheer drop off both sides into the canyon below. It can be a heart-stopping moment when a deer is trapped in the circle by approaching tourists, and suddenly leaps over the railing. A peek over the edge, though, reveals a few yards of scree-covered terrain before the outcrop slopes away down a tree-dotted ridge. Deer, birds and rodents frequent the area, no doubt scrounging scraps from the two-legged interlopers. Traffic is usually pretty light by late afternoon, and you may even have the overlook to yourself. That is, until a few dozen chipmunks appear and close in like so many Dickensian street urchins, sometimes crawling from the rock wall you're leaning on right up your sleeve to mooch a handout. Brother, can you spare a Corn Nut?

Staying open to possibility and being willing to follow your curiosity are key to getting the most out of a cruise over the Beartooth Highway, the preferred road through Yellowstone Country for many. Whether you're coming from a Yellowstone excursion or making the Beartooth a standalone adventure, this amazing journey will provide enough beauty and dramatic scenery to make you eager to come back for another spin.

THE MYSTERY OF THE WHIRLING RAINBOWS

FLY FISHING IS TANTAMOUNT TO RELIGION in Montana, and more than two million wader-clad worshipers ply its lakes, streams and rivers every year. Anglers testified to the tune of $919.3 million in 2017, and the latest numbers show the industry provides between 50,000 and 70,000 jobs. Thanks to careful regulation and management by the state of its many fisheries, the overall health of Montana's trout population is excellent.

Except when it's not. In the early 1990s the fishing community was sent into near-panic when something called Whirling Disease took hold in the upper Madison River, considered by many to be the finest piece of fly-fishing water in North America. Alarmingly, the disease attacked only rainbow trout, Montana's number one gamefish. When infected by a microscopic parasite that carried the disease, it would attack the spinal column, causing the fish to swim in tight circles—giving the disease its name— and soon die. By 1998, ninety percent of the upper Madison's rainbow trout were wiped out. Fish counts showed fewer than 120 adult rainbows per mile, where 3,000 total fish was the norm. There were also signs that the disease appeared to be spreading to other tributaries. Biologists were stumped. Could the outbreak be stopped? Would other species be affected? For a few years, the possibility loomed that Montana's prestigious trout fishing culture, and the industry it supported, could collapse.

Rainbows weren't always prevalent in Montana. When the transcontinental railroad arrived and opened up the West in the 1880s, bull trout and cutthroat were the only native trout in the Northern Rockies. Not a single rainbow trout lived in the waters of Montana. As easterners began to visit the region in larger numbers, "bucket biologists" began stocking the new waters with trout native to the eastern U.S. and their homelands—European species like German browns, brook trout, and lake trout. Immigrating sportsmen dumped egg slurry into the river systems across Colorado, Utah, Montana, and other states hoping to expand the variety of gamefish in the new territory. While the browns, brookies, and lake trout came from the east, rainbow trout were brought in from California. Rainbows proved to be hardy and less wary than other trout, and became known for their acrobatic displays when hooked. As the various imported trout became established in watersheds across the west, rainbow trout quickly became one of the most popular gamefish.

Rainbow trout were on the verge of extirpation on the upper Madison River in the 1990s. Photo courtesy of 123rf.com © goodluz

"It was a Johnny Appleseed mentality," Bob Behnke, a fisheries professor from Colorado State University, said in a 1995 interview. "They scattered fish around, thinking they'd end up with more fish, but no consideration (was given to) the ecosystem. They thought they could do better than nature." The introduced species were aggressive, and soon dominated the habitat, feeding on the fry and eggs of native trout. The introduction of those species pointed to the major problems that could result when humans attempted to improve on nature. Today, for instance, non-native lake trout currently dominate the aquatic ecosystem of Flathead Lake, and are well on their way to displacing the highly valued native cutthroat population in Yellowstone Lake. Although Wyoming and Montana are pouring millions of dollars into trying to reverse the lake trout takeover, it might be an unwinnable battle. Whirling disease was yet another symptom—it seemed—of the best of intentions going awry. "Truthfully," says biologist Dick Vincent, "it would have been better to leave the cutthroats here, and not bring in the rainbows and browns, but that decision was made for us in the 1880s. Once you bring in the exotics, you're hung."

Vincent has spent more than 40 years studying the Madison River. A senior fisheries biologist with Montana's Fish, Wildlife & Parks Dept., he feared the worst when the outbreak was discovered. "We thought the river was in real trouble. The theory was that it would take hundreds of years or even longer (for the species to recover), because the assumption was that there was no inherent resistance." As it turned out, however, except for a few outliers, Whirling Disease affected only rainbow trout, and scientists soon determined the reason: The parasite that caused the disease came from European trout. Those fish had plenty of time to develop a genetic resistance to the disease. The California-bred rainbows never had a chance. Most trout species spawn in the fall. When their eggs hatch in February the river waters are too cold to support the tubifex worms that expel waterborne tractinomyxons, or TAMs. Rainbow trout, on the other hand, spawn in the spring and their fry hatch in early summer when water temperatures are warmer and the tubifex worms are active.

The ongoing investigation revealed that the introduction of the parasite, *Myxobolus cerebralis,* to the U.S. can be traced to a single source. In 1957 a shipment of frozen trout from Denmark that had been infected with Whirling Disease was ground up and fed to thousands of trout in a Pennsylvania hatchery. Over time, they worked their way out West. In their microscopic spore form, the parasites are virtually indestructible. They can freeze, they can withstand punishing heat, they can lie dormant indefinitely until they're ingested by the bottom-dwelling tubifex worm, and then be excreted as TAMs. The buoyant parasites float downstream, attach themselves to trout and attack the nervous system, moving up the spine to the cartilage of the head. An infected trout's tail will usually turn black, and damage to the spinal column renders the fish unable to swim straight, causing them to swim in tail-chasing circles.

Throughout the mid-90s, Whirling Disease dominated the headlines as the disease continued to spread. Senator Max Baucus declared a national emergency and introduced the Whirling Disease Response Act of 1995. "Fishing is big business," said Baucus. "It is the engine that drives the economies of many communities throughout Montana." Rainbow trout—plentiful, fun to catch and tasty to eat—are the most popular trout in Montana's waters. If their population couldn't be saved, many wondered, would they take Montana's trout fishing industry down with them?

Efforts to reverse, or even isolate, the disease didn't seem to be working. In 1998 infected trout were found in Little Prickly Pear Creek, a major spawning tributary of the Missouri. Three years later the disease was found on the Dearborn River, another, larger tributary. Although Montana had not stocked its streams and rivers for forty years, there was talk of a hatchery-based solution to replace the rainbows. Biologists could trap the remaining natives on the Madison—the resistant ones—and strip them of their eggs and sperm to create a disease-resistant designer trout. Ultimately, that plan was scrapped and the decision was made to let nature take its course, and hope for the best.

The story has a more-or-less happy ending. The hands-off approach gave the rainbows the chance to recover on their own, which they did through a combination of genetic development and their selection of superior spawning grounds. Some tributaries, like Sheep Creek off the Dearborn River, were free of the disease, and their isolation from the affected waters may have helped slow its spread. Another contributing factor is the genetic diversity of a mainstem spawning area like the Missouri River, which contributes to a more disease-resistant strain of trout. Today's rainbow trout population in the Madison are likely descendants of those hardy few who survived the original outbreak.

The rainbows are back, but Whirling Disease is here to stay. The spore is carried by healthy trout much like humans carry the cold virus. When the fish are stressed, due to low oxygen or high-water temps as found in late summer, their systems are weakened and they become susceptible to infection. With additional factors like agricultural runoff, bank erosion from development near streams, and the residual effects of climate change like more frequent flooding and higher water temperatures, another outbreak is not out of the question. Whether it's contained to the waters of Yellowstone Country or pops up elsewhere in the state, Whirling Disease is one of the problems that can be traced directly to America's colonization of the West that brought with it a rash of environmental issues that would continue to bedevil Montana for generations.

COWBOYS AND INDIANS: THE PLIGHT OF THE YELLOWSTONE BISON

IT MAY BE HARD TO FATHOM while viewing a thousand or so bison gathered along a stretch of the Lamar River on the northern tier of Yellowstone National Park, but these impressive animals have bounced back from the very edge of extinction. Due to unchecked poaching in the park, by 1902 only two dozen bison were left in Yellowstone's Pelican Valley, all that remained of the original herd. Through aggressive conservation efforts, careful management and swift congressional action thanks in part to conservationist Theodore Roosevelt, Yellowstone's pure strain of bison, a species that's been around since prehistoric times, has rebounded to the healthy numbers of today. Currently around 4,500 of the shaggy beasts roam the landscape of the park, descendants of that original herd. The two main herds congregate in the north, from the park entrance at Gardiner to the Lamar Valley, and in the Hayden Valley just north of Yellowstone Lake. Bison roam throughout the park, though, from the boardwalks of the Upper Geyser Basin to the Madison Valley along the river leading from West Yellowstone.

In the area surrounding the park, however, the bison has become a victim of its own success. The cattle industry, which has been prevalent in the West for only about 150 years, has found itself in direct conflict with our national mammal. The vast grasslands that were once the domain of tens of millions of bison are now dominated by beef cattle, and ranchers are fighting efforts to reestablish bison herds outside the park. Besides competing for grazing lands, many bison carry brucellosis, a bacterial disease that can cause calves to be stillborn. Although the disease can be transmitted from bison to elk, there are no recorded cases of brucellosis being transmitted directly from bison to cows in the wild. Still, the cattle industry is largely opposed to bison coming anywhere near their livelihood.

"Trying to bring back the buffalo in big herds across Montana is like bringing back dinosaurs," says State Senator John Brendan, who introduced a bill that would allow

Hundreds of Yellowstone bison are captured outside the park and sent to slaughter each year, partly to maintain a population balance within the park.
Photo courtesy of 123rf.com © Paul Tessier

landowners to shoot bison that enter their property. "And who wants dinosaurs in Montana? I certainly don't."

Bison do not, of course, recognize the artificial boundaries that separate Yellowstone Park from its surrounding environs. As they follow their ancestral migration paths along the Madison and Yellowstone Rivers, the moment they set foot across that border into Gardiner or West Yellowstone they are no longer under the park's protection. Over the last few years, thousands of bison have been killed by hunters and government agents after wandering out of Yellowstone, while hundreds more are hazed back into the park with helicopters and ATVs. The fate of these migrating bison has created a management quagmire involving the livestock industry, the state's Indian nations, the hunting community, environmentalists, and a growing conservation movement called the American Prairie Reserve, which has established a herd of more than 800 bison in north-central Montana.

After a decade of negotiations and lawsuits, the Interagency Bison Management Plan (IBMP) was introduced in 2000 with the goal of responsibly managing the Yellowstone bison in and around the park. The plan involves the National Park Service, USDA-Forest Service, USDA-Animal & Plant Health Inspection Service (APHIS), Montana Department of Livestock and Montana Fish Wildlife & Parks. These government agencies have been working with several Montana tribes for nearly two decades to hammer out agreements and details that would eventually allow herds of Yellowstone bison to be established on the Reservations, while providing management of the animals that wander out of the park. With so many entities coming at the problem from divergent directions, it's a hot-button issue with no clear path forward.

Bison ranches are scattered across Montana, but those domesticated herds contain some genetic material from cattle, with which they've been cross-bred for decades. It's the genetically pure Yellowstone herd, direct descendants of the original population that filled the plain of the West up until their near-extinction in the 1870s, that is causing most of the hand-wringing.

On the Fort Belknap Reservation, located forty miles south of the Canadian border in north-central Montana, a herd of Yellowstone bison has already been established. In August of 2013, after spending time quarantined at the Fort Peck Indian Reservation, 34 genetically pure bison trotted off trailers onto tribal lands inhabited by the Assiniboine and Gros Ventre. It took Montana's Supreme Court lifting a lower court's injunction to allow delivery of the bison. Now it's up to Fort Belknap's tribes to provide management for the bison that have been returned to their original habitat.

At Fort Peck Reservation, the Assiniboine and Sioux are ready to establish their own herd of Yellowstone bison, but have become entangled in legal and policy imbroglios surrounding the quarantine process the bison must go through to ensure they don't carry brucellosis. Most recently, the federal government has been unwilling to let the tribes perform all three phases of assurance testing on bison quarantined in Fort Peck's own facility, which has frustrated tribal members who feel the government is overstepping its bounds.

"I don't understand why we have IBMP," said Majel Russell, legal counsel for the Assiniboine and Sioux tribes. "We're not willing to sign an agreement that boxes only into assurance testing. This is the group that should be making the decisions."

The Montana Department of Livestock disagrees, insisting that the Yellowstone bison undergo brucellosis testing at their Stephens Creek facility before they are allowed to be moved to Fort Peck, although that facility is already operating at capacity. "We want to maintain confidence in the bisons' brucellosis-free status," said Mike Honeycutt of the Montana Board of Livestock. "The state eagerly awaits resolution between APHIS and Fort Peck."

Tribal members have harvested some of the bison as they've left the park, and have been allowed to process the animals using their cultural techniques and ceremonies. Culling hunts have been held, with bison being shot by sportsmen the moment they leave the park. The legal settlement that led to the creation of the IBMP arrived at a target population of 3,000 bison within the park, a figure considered to be a sustainable sweet spot for the health and propagation of the genetically pure herd. As the population currently hovers near 5,000, hundreds of bison are killed as they leave the park. The bisons' added pressure on grazing lands—although they are far less destructive than cattle—in addition to fears of the spread of brucellosis drive the cattle industry to keep the pressure on Fish, Wildlife and Parks and other agencies to control their movements outside Yellowstone. In 2018 more than 1,100 bison that wandered outside the park were slaughtered. Although "tolerance zones" have been created that allow for some back-and-forth travel around Yellowstone's northwest corner, many bison still travel beyond these areas, directly into the crosshairs of the anti-bison faction.

As for the future of Yellowstone's thriving bison herd, more quarantine facilities are in the works, and park officials are hopeful that the original Yellowstone herd can eventually be established on Montana's tribal lands, where massive armies of buffalo once rumbled across the open prairie as far as the eye could see.

The 3D International Restaurant in Black Eagle has been a popular haunt for locals since 1946.

TASTING THE BIG SKY

I should write a book about writing this book. My research produced some pretty interesting stories. As convenient as it is to access a thousand libraries' worth of reference materials online from home, I couldn't hope to get a real handle on these diverse regions of Montana without physically being there. Some things just have to be seen, felt, heard and smelled. With that in mind, I spent six months, to paraphrase the old Del Reeves song, looking at Montana through a windshield.

I camped a lot, which entailed bringing a cooler stuffed with sandwich fixin's and easy meals, but I also seized the opportunity to sample the local fare whenever I could. In this section I'll share some of those meals with you, although my best efforts at description won't be able to capture the experience in all its exotic glory. When you're on the road, even a basic cheeseburger can be a singular pleasure because of the context.

Speaking of burgers, I can't pass up a good buffalo burger, and it seems the closer I find myself to Yellowstone Park, the stronger the craving gets. Native Americans were onto something here. Bison meat is super lean, lower in calories and fat than ground beef, and higher in protein. And it's delicious. Montana boasts several buffalo ranches that raise the animals for meat, and they're virtually all grass-fed. Their organic production and lower consumer demand means buffalo meat costs about twice as much as beef, but for a single burger, that might translate to just a couple of dollars. My first buffalo burger was consumed about ten years ago in Gardiner on the way into Yellowstone Park. I'd stopped at a restaurant situated beneath a two-story sign that said, "EAT" in big, red letters. When in Rome, I thought, and ordered the buffalo burger. What I got made a McDonald's hamburger look like filet mignon. The thin, gray disc between the sad buns was burnt on the edges and yet still cool in the middle, and had the flavor profile of a potholder. It may have been yak, for all I know. I didn't bother to ask. As I sat there gnawing on the disappointing patty, watching buffalo walking around in the park across the street, the lesson was clear: Never eat at the restaurant that has the biggest sign.

Fast forward to 2017. I'm in West Yellowstone for a few days, traveling alone. After a day in the park, I slid onto a barstool at the Slippery Otter, ordered a Bozone beer and a bison burger. The hand-formed patty was juicy and well-seasoned, accompanied by excellent hand-cut fries. The servers and bartender obviously enjoyed working there and were full of little-known tidbits about Yellowstone. That was a tasty burger.

The best buffalo burger I've had to date was found in a small cafe in Darby, not far north of Idaho on State Highway 93 South. Their portions would have satisfied an NFL linebacker, and the bison burger was no exception. "The Buffalo Trapper" wasn't just a burger, it was a commitment. The half-pound burger was stacked tall with red onion, lettuce, tomato and god knows what else on a well-toasted bun. This thing took me three sessions to finish. It was gloriously sloppy, loaded with flavor, and just everything a bison burger could be. The price was around $20, but that's not bad for three meals.

Another notable repast featured another of Montana's celebrated wild game, the rainbow trout. My wife and I had snagged a cabin one summer weekend in Silver Gate, just outside Yellowstone's northeast entrance. We

"Brent's Classic Cheddar" is one of the more conventional offerings on Parker's Family Restaurant's 136-item burger menu.

asked the cabin proprietor for a dinner recommendation, and she pointed to the tiny cafe next door. It was the only restaurant in town, and the front window was aglow with a large neon sign that read, "Fresh Rainbow Trout." We went in, grabbed a table and ordered the trout, which was butterflied and pan-fried. The service was indifferent, the side dishes forgettable, and the atmosphere had all the charm of a Wendy's. But oh, that trout! I would have eaten it off a paper plate sitting on an upturned garbage can in the alley. It was magnificent. Firm, sweet meat perfectly breaded—but not too heavily—

in a nicely seasoned cornmeal/flour dredge. Butterflying opens up the fish, allowing both sides of each filet to be cooked to a crispy, perfectly browned crunch. The bones were easily picked out of the flesh, and a single bite of the wild-caught fish zoomed my memory back to when I was a small boy, learning to catch rainbow trout at the Nevada Creek Dam near Helmville. My father had a cast iron skillet popping with oil over a small fire in the rocks of the dam, and we cooked and ate several trout as soon as they were caught and cleaned. Some tastes and smells have the power to turn your memory into a time machine, and this butterflied trout at the Log Cabin Cafe in Silver Gate was loaded with it. We ate there twice.

The bison burger at Foster & Logan's in Red Lodge was a little dry (that's on me because I used zero condiments), but I poached a few bites from my wife's meal, their Philly cheese steak, which she'd ordered sans bun. The thin-sliced ribeye was perfectly grilled, nicely complemented by the rich gouda cheese sauce. I even enjoyed the roasted bell peppers, which I've spurned since I was a kid. After a couple of microbrews I was ready to put my whole face into her plate.

In Custer Country, the bean soup at the Jersey Lilly in Ingomar stands out as a filling, delicious experience to break up a long drive along Highway 12. And I recommend you start things off with the Sheepherder's hors d'oeuvres. It's a surprise party in your mouth.

After a day of sampling wild game dishes at the Hunters Feed in Ennis, I reveled in the blessed relief (I am not a fan of wild game) of a huge plate of fettuccine alfredo at the bar in the Sportsman's Lodge, where I shared a fascinating conversation with an old cowboy who used to be a surfer.

I plowed through a generous homestyle breakfast at the Wagon Wheel Cafe in Ekalaka, while I listened to Dave, a compact rancher wearing a Filson vest over a denim shirt buttoned at the wrists, describe the 30-foot drifts he encountered during their long winters. His stories of unfortunate people who'd frozen to death in the harsh environs were so engrossing that I inadvertently left the Wagon Wheel without paying my bill (I later mailed them a check).

I munched a huge, crisp and complicated salad on the Hi-Line in Chester one afternoon, and took a hard look at my own racial bias after doing a double take when I saw a black man tending bar. At Indian Days in Browning, after a day of interviewing tribal members about their experiences with bigotry, I bought an Indian taco that had me emptying my guts into a campground vault toilet 12 hours later, which had me wondering if I was paying some kind of penance for my own white privilege. Turns out I'd just bought the food from a vendor who hadn't kept their chili at proper temperature.

Like I say, these meals weren't just fuel for my body. They were an important part of the overall travel experience, and they all added in their own way to the identity of the particular region of Montana where I'd (in most cases) enjoyed them. You might be able to save a few bucks by bringing your own provisions, but it would be a big mistake to do any traveling in Montana and pass up the chance to taste some of the state for yourself.

*The Marias River flows eastward through the Tiber Reservoir,
then joins up with the Missouri River at Loma.*

RUSSELL COUNTRY

PERHAPS MORE THAN ANY OF MONTANA'S six regions, Russell Country resembles a microcosm of the state itself. There are mountains to the west, prairies and badlands in the east, and they share a long border with Canada to the north. Historically, this is the land of some heavy hitters who give the rest of Montana much of its cultural identity. Geographically and symbolically, Russell Country is very much the heart of Montana.

Black Eagle Dam, Montana's first hydroelectric dam, gives Great Falls its nickname of "Electric City."
Photo © Troy Schlimgen

As it does in much of Montana, agriculture drives the economy here. Winter wheat accounts for 2.25 million acres of Montana farmland, bringing some half a billion dollars in at harvest. The Golden Triangle—its three points being Conrad, Havre and Great Falls—is one of the most productive of those wheat-growing areas, and throughout the summer those amber waves of grain stretch from the edge of the Northern Front eastward for hundreds of miles. Farmers and ranchers up here are a hard-working but mostly affable bunch. They can be found clustered in ranch town coffee shops early in the day, sharing scuttlebutt and swapping knowledge about all things agribusiness. Lately the conversations are peppered with grizzly sightings, as the bear population rebounds and they expand their range. It's a recent development that's cause for concern for ranchers, some of whom are losing stock animals to the apex predators.

Russell Country has its urban side, of course, with Great Falls, population 58,876, serving as the hub. Since 1939 it's been the home of Malmstrom Air Force Base, which is the command for the U.S. Intercontinental Ballistic Missile Program, a Cold War-era defense system that maintains more than 150 ICBM launch facilities scattered throughout a 23,500 square mile area. The missiles are currently decommissioned. Elsewhere in Great Falls is another Russell Country claim to fame: The Sip 'n Dip, Montana's only mermaid bar. Piano Pat, a Great Falls legend, plays pop favorites there several nights a week, as she has done for more than 50 years, while mermaids and mermen undulate in the pool, entertaining patrons through a glass wall behind the bar. Up the road in Havre, the city offers a fair amount of Montana art and history, as well as an important piece of Native American history at the Wahkpa Chu'gn buffalo jump site. Just south of Havre, the eastern point of the Golden Triangle, is Big Sandy, a little farming community that has produced a U.S. Senator (Jon Tester) and a Rock and Roll Hall of Famer (Jeff Ament of Pearl Jam). Both still maintain homes in Montana.

Speaking of history, even though it's called Russell Country after the famous western painter Charlie Russell, explorers Lewis and Clark seem to get more of the limelight. Their Corps of Discovery cut right through the region and that famous expedition is commemorated here perhaps more than anywhere else in Montana. History buffs absolutely should not miss the Lewis and Clark Interpretive Center, one of the most attractive regional museums in the state. Perched on a cliff overlooking the Missouri River just downstream from the Black Eagle Falls, the museum is a great place to peruse the exhibits and take in some of Montana's fascinating history. Looking out the large windows over the spectacular falls and the massive buttes scattered in the distance, it's not hard to imagine why so many people, from the pioneer days to now, decide to put down roots in Russell Country.

THIS LEGEND OF THE WEST
WORE A DRESS

OUT ON THE WESTERN EDGE OF RUSSELL COUNTRY, north of Helena and west of Eden (sorry, John Steinbeck), the tiny town of Cascade lies along the west bank of the Missouri River. While erstwhile resident C. M. Russell was traveling around the area creating his iconic paintings of the West, a unique woman was building a legend of her own. In the late 1800s through the early part of the twentieth century, Cascade's most beloved and notorious resident was a former slave from Tennessee who went by the moniker Stagecoach Mary. Some knew her as Black Mary. Quick with a gun, Mary Fields was a tall brickhouse without fear of man nor beast. She loved nothing more than tipping back a few whiskeys while enjoying a good cigar. To paraphrase James Brown, Black Mary didn't take no mess. So how did this African-American flower of the South wind up running one of Montana's toughest mail routes with her whiskey-drinking pet eagle on her arm and a well-used six-gun in her belt? As with many of Montana's pioneers, her journey west began with the Civil War.

Born into a Tennessee slave family in 1832, Mary eventually moved into the main house and worked for the white Dunne family, becoming close with Dolly Dunne, who was the same age as she. The two friends were split apart when, at sixteen, Dolly was sent off to an Ursuline boarding school in Ohio where she would study to become a nun.

Mary, by the time she was twenty, had grown into a formidable woman. Six feet tall and two hundred pounds, she'd developed a taste for moonshine and tobacco, and had acquired sufficient carpentry skills to build a chicken coop so she could supply the farm with eggs and poultry. She'd also learned to read and write, a rare distinction among slaves. A few years after Dolly left, Mary's mother died, and she was put in charge of the slaves. Her no-nonsense approach to running the farm won the respect of her fellow slaves as well as the rest of the Dunne family.

When the Civil War erupted in 1861 the farm fell into turmoil as the soldiers stripped the farm of most of its resources to support the war effort. What little they left behind was soon pilfered by the Union men, and the slaves were left to subsist on their meager garden production and what little game they could kill. Finally, the Emancipation Proclamation swept through the South as the Civil War ended. Mary was 33 years old, all freed up and no place to go.

Meanwhile, Dolly Dunne, now known as Mother Amadeus, had been working at
the Ursuline convent in Toledo. When the Dunne family sold what was left of their
war-ravaged farm, Dolly sent for her old friend. Mary's impact on the lives of the
nuns was immediate. Her skills in the kitchen improved the food, and she immediately constructed a chicken coop and planted a vegetable garden, much to the delight
of the Ursuline sisters. She even added a couple of pigs to the mix, explaining with
typical Black Mary pragmatism, "What people don't eat, pigs and chickens eat. Then
we eat them." Although the sisters knew she was sneaking sips of whiskey and puffs
of cigars in the henhouse, they looked the other way. Mary was heaven sent—she
could do it all.

It was around this time that Jesuit priests shifted into high gear with their assim-
ilation efforts in the American West. Intrepid Christians were dispatched to set up
church schools where they would gather Indian children, typically separating them
from their families that were being forced onto reservations and supplanting their
Native traditions and spiritualism with the dogma of the European church. Mother
Amadeus headed west in 1884 to join a Montana school, and Mary wasn't far behind.
At St. Peter's Mission near Cascade, Mary put her stamp on the settlement right
away with a chicken coop and garden. She repaired furniture, painted buildings, and
learned how to tan hides for buckskin.

In 1885 Mary, then 54, would make an unlikely but loyal friend at St. Peter's Mission. Mary Wells, age seven, arrived at the mission school with her two brothers. Her
father was white, but her mother was a Gros Ventre tribal member, and the children
had been sent to the mission to have their Indian identity worked out of them. This

ethnic whitewashing infuriated Mary Fields, bringing back memories of her young life among the slaves, how their African heritage was beaten out of them by their white overseers. The two Marys became good friends, the young girl shadowing the tall, cantankerous black woman in the buckskin dress as she moved about the mission, fixing this and building that.

As the years passed, Mary Fields assumed the position of forewoman, although her authority was constantly challenged by the white laborers hired to work at the mission. Eventually one of these conflicts pushed Mary over the line, and she shot a man who had threatened her life. This proved to be too much for the local diocese, who, over the protests of the nuns and few of the Jesuit priests, banished Mary from St. Peter's Mission.

By this time Black Mary's reputation preceded her, and she was able to secure a mail route in Cascade. Only the second woman to run a mail route in the country, she was the first black woman to do so. During her time at the mission she'd rescued an injured bald eagle and nursed it back to health, naming it Bird. She brought Bird with her to Cascade, and Mary cut quite a figure as she traveled the rutted trails of Russell Country, Bird perched beside her as she delivered mail and warded off trouble with her ever-present shotgun and six-shooter. Stagecoach Mary, as she came to be known, still liked her cigars and whiskey and could frequently be found kicked back in a dusty saloon, eagle by her chair, playing cards and holding her own among the crusty denizens of the West.

By 1900 she had been in Montana for fifteen years, and had seen a lifetime's worth of adventure, joy and sorrow. Bird died in 1901 and soon after that Mary quit her mail route. Not suited to the stasis of retirement, she began taking in washing and opened a small eatery in Cascade. Although she was a scrupulous businesswoman, her big heart was Mary's Achilles heel. Her habit of extending credit to anyone who didn't have the money to pay for a meal would be the eventual undoing of her eatery. Her generosity didn't extend to welshers, however. Legend has it that once, while drinking in a saloon, Mary spotted a customer who had stiffed her for two dollars on his laundry bill. She followed him out into the street and dropped him with a single punch. Wiping her hands on her apron, she walked back into the saloon and announced, "That debt is paid."

As tough as she was, even Mary would eventually begin to slow down, and after she retired from her mail route the bad news began to pile up. She'd kept in touch with Mary Wells, who had married a Jesuit from St. Peter's named Joseph Gump and moved to Havre, which was close enough to Cascade for the occasional visit. But the Gumps, she learned in July of 1902, were moving to Spokane. That was farther than she cared to travel, so she knew she'd never see her old friends Mary and Joseph again. Later that year old friend Dolly was seriously injured in a train wreck in Billings, and the following year moved to California to recuperate. Mary had never gotten around to starting a family of her own, and she found herself more alone than ever.

In 1908 a fire destroyed part of her beloved St. Peter's Mission, which she still visited once a year from her home in Cascade. A plan was made to move the Mission to a more accessible location in Great Falls, and Mary was asked to move there to help establish the new school. She declined, admitting that she was too frail to travel.

Stagecoach Mary Fields fell ill in 1914 and died in a Great Falls hospital, but not before being immortalized in a C. M. Russell sketch titled, "A Quiet Day in Cascade." It depicts a frenetic scene of Cascadians going about their day, with Mary Fields hopping mad as a mule kicks over her basket of eggs. It's a fitting depiction of the plucky ex-slave whose life was a nonstop parade of challenges overcome. Stagecoach Mary, aka Black Mary, aka Mary Fields overcame them with style. A granite headstone marks her grave in a small cemetery outside of Cascade, on a dirt road that leads to St. Peter's Mission.

FIRST PEOPLES BUFFALO JUMP STATE PARK

WHAT'S THE EASIEST WAY TO KILL a herd of buffalo? For Montana's Plains Indians, the answer was simple: Pursuade them to kill themselves. For almost a thousand years, Native Americans in Montana used *pishkun*, or buffalo jumps, sites where herds of buffalo would be driven over a cliff to fall to their deaths, sometimes hundreds at a time. Before the advent of the horse, this was the most efficient method to provide tribes with meat, tools, clothing, and other essentials that were harvested from the animal that was such an integral part of their existence, both literally and spiritually. Several buffalo jump sites have been identified in Montana, including the Madison Buffalo Jump in Gallatin County, the Wahkpa Chu'gn Buffalo Jump in Havre, and what may be the world's largest buffalo jump, Ulm Pishkun at Peoples Buffalo Jump near Great Falls.

Although the mile-long cliff at Ulm Pishkun was located in Blackfeet territory, the site was used by at least a dozen tribes. Oral histories of tribes that frequented the buffalo jump suggest that, as with other sacred sites that provided resources to many Northern Plains tribes, Ulm Pishkun was understood to be a non-warring area. The Assiniboine, Nez Perce, Crow, Shoshone, Gros Ventre and other tribes all were known to harvest buffalo at Ulm Pishkun at various times, co-existing peacefully while there. The site was the perfect combination of geological features to execute a successful buffalo jump. The

Square Butte can be seen in the distance from the First Peoples Buffalo Jump at Ulm Pishkun.

sandstone cliff is fifty feet tall at its highest point, and it lay along the edge of miles of gently rolling grassland, prime habitat for bison. Archaeologists have found bones and artifacts that show Indians began using the buffalo jump here about 900 years ago.

The terms "bison" and "buffalo" are used interchangeably, although the animal is technically the North American bison. They are smart, ornery, and sometimes unpredictable. So, how do you persuade a few hundred of them to voluntarily run off a cliff to certain death? In order to outsmart a buffalo, you have to think like a buffalo, and there was no one more versed in buffalo behavior than the North American Indian. Oral histories present the fascinating concept of a young Native male luring the animals *en masse* over the edge of a cliff. The process was long and complex and began with the selection and grooming of an adolescent boy who had bested his peers in foot races and games of skill, and had demonstrated a deep knowledge of buffalo behavior. A tribe's buffalo runner was a coveted and prestigious job, and it required someone who was not only brave and crafty, but selfless—the chosen young man would risk his life for the good of the tribe.

The buffalo runner and his crew would locate a herd, sometimes several days' journey from the tribe's encampment, and observe the animals long enough to identify the leader, typically an older cow with no calves of her own. The runner would rub himself with sage to disguise his scent, cover up with a buffalo robe, and slowly move toward the herd. Buffalo are nearsighted, so the runner maintained his distance, coming just close enough to the herd to be mistaken for a calf. After the herd's leader checked to see that all of the herd's young had been accounted for, she would have moved toward the runner to bring him back to the herd. As she followed the runner, the herd followed her. It was a slow process that demanded patience and stamina. Meanwhile drive lanes had been constructed closer to the jump, using rocks, sticks and buffalo dung to create walls that would guide the herd toward the cliff. Once the herd has begun to move, some men would don wolf skins and get behind them to keep the animals moving forward. Indians hiding behind the drive lane walls waved feathers and other objects to keep the bison in the lane. As the herd finally got within range of the cliff, the runner would drop his robe and run straight to the cliff's edge. The lead buffalo gave chase. The herd would run obediently after her, pounding the ground, filling the air with dust. Visibility became limited, and the animals had no idea they were heading for the precipice. As the runner reached the cliff, the lead bison hot on his heels, he would drop over the edge and land a few feet below on a predetermined ledge of rock. By now the herd could not stop. Pushed forward by the rampaging buffalo in the rear, the entire herd poured off the cliff and plummeted to the rocky terrain below. Typically, a few buffalo would survive after landing on a pile of their dead companions, so a few people, mostly women and children, were posted at the bottom with spears to finish them off. Natives believed that if a buffalo did survive the fall and managed to escape, it would convey its knowledge of the buffalo jump technique to other herds and they would become wise to the Indians' chicanery and not allow themselves to fall for the buffalo-runner-in-the-robe trick.

The buffalo jump was one of the most dramatic and most productive rituals of Indian culture, and First Peoples Buffalo Jump State Park is an excellent site to learn about it. There is a first-rate visitor's center less than half a mile from the base of the cliff, and it offers capsule histories of the tribes known to have used the jump, and features a detailed diorama of a tepee site, including mounts of several local species of birds and terrestrial animals. Outside, a broad trail runs from the center past a few tepees, up the grassland slope, where it narrows and winds along the face of the cliff, eventually leading up and onto the plateau above. On the trail just below the cliff, tiny pieces of white buffalo bone are visible, scattered in the dirt. The animals had to be processed on the spot to keep the meat from spoiling, and only their bones were left behind as Natives had a use for virtually every part of the buffalo. Archaeological excavations in the early twentieth century revealed pits full of bones and other materials more than a dozen feet deep at the base of the cliff. The area was actually mined for buffalo bone in the mid-1940s to use as fertilizer, but its significance as a cultural site was eventually recognized. Now it's illegal to remove any piece of buffalo bone or other artifact found at the site.

A road circles around the area on the upper bench and leads to a small parking lot just a few hundred yards from the cliff, overlooking a broad expanse of Russell Country. You can pick up the trail there and head down to the visitors center below, or you can linger a while, perhaps look off toward the Rocky Mountain Front and see the impressive silhouette of Crown Butte. It's easy to imagine a tribe gathered down below, thanking the Creator while waiting for a herd of snorting, bellowing buffalo to pour over the edge of the precipice. There's a quiet sense of reverence up there on that cliff, a powerful calm that invites respect for both the Native Americans and the buffalo that sustained them. It's also a powerful reminder that the rich land that supports the farms and ranches that surround Ulm Pishkin have a history that's deeper than that of the Montanans who work that land today.

HAVRE AND THE RES:
TWO CULTURES AT A CROSSROADS

JUST 35 MILES SOUTH OF THE CANADIAN BORDER. Havre sits on the Milk River halfway across Montana on the Hi-Line, the relentlessly straight stretch of State Highway 2 running between Browning and Culbertson, paralleled by the main line of the Burlington Northern and Santa Fe railroad. If the Hi-Line, as they say, is just a small town with a really long Main Street, then Havre would probably be City Hall. The pretty river town of 10,000 is a stop on the Amtrak route, and most folks here, as in other small Montana towns, seem open and friendly.

Forty-four miles to the east of Havre is the Fort Belknap reservation, home to about seven thousand members of the Assiniboine and Gros Ventre tribes. Rocky Boy, the smallest of Montana's seven Indian reservations, lies about ten miles south of Havre on State Highway 87. There are 3,323 tribal members on Rocky Boy, most of them Chippewa Cree.

Due largely to their proximity to each other and the vast distances between towns in northeast Montana, this triangle of communities are economically intertwined. This is farm and ranch country, endless plains punctuated by rolling hills and the occasional creek. The Milk River bounds the region to the north, the Bears Paw Mountains to the south. Havre takes pride in its agricultural heritage, and there's a certain austere beauty here that seems to suggest a Montana frozen in time, a place that is resistant to change. The old ways run deep in Havre, and that's one of the town's biggest attractions. It's also its worst problem.

With scant consumer opportunity on the reservations, tribal members spend the bulk of their income in Havre. The town depends on the people from the reservations as much as they depend on the town. A Havre business owner puts it bluntly: "Without business from the tribes, Havre would dry up and blow away." And yet, for generations, Native Americans who visit, work, live and shop in Havre have felt the baleful gaze of racism from the very people whose livelihoods they support.

Many who live on the Fort Belknap and Rocky Boy Reservations, as well as in Havre, feel that younger generations are developing a world view that will help eliminate racism between whites and Native Americans in Montana.
Photo © Jonathan Qualben

"I'll shop in Great Falls rather than put up with the racist vibe in Havre," says Raymond "Jazz" Parker, the Native American manager of Northern Winz casino, a ten minute drive from Havre on the Rocky Boy reservation. In the aisles of Havre's Walmart, he says, white hatred toward Native Americans is right out in the open. "People are screaming and yelling at each other." Parker recently returned from living out of state to manage the casino, one of the largest in the region. "I was gone thirteen years. Nothing's really changed."

Fifteen percent of the students who attend MSU-Northern in Havre are Native American, more than twice the average of Montana's state colleges, but its larger Native presence in what one would assume is a more enlightened academic setting doesn't seem to have done much to stem the racism occasionally revealed by some white students. In 2017 a young white man was removed from the school after he was overheard commenting about disliking his Native American Studies class, and how if the Indians had been wiped out there would be no reason for it. His casual mention of genocide had some students fearing for their lives. Yvonne Tiger, a Native American faculty member, filed a complaint with the Montana Human Rights Bureau.

A Native business owner in Havre (who asked not to be identified) agrees that the racism displayed toward the Indian population is rampant, and Indians doing business in Havre can feel it. "It's like a birthmark that's real prominent on your face. Everybody knows about it but they avoid mentioning it." The business owner adds that it's gotten noticeably worse since the 2016 election. "Racists are ruffling their feathers. They're driving up and down Main Street with Confederate flags flying." Mention is made of some non-native people who came into the business and told the business owner not to sell the merchandise—native art—in Havre, suggesting the Indians "keep this stuff on the res."

Racism in an institutional form also reaches deep into the reservation, even when white people are nowhere to be found. In fact, that's kind of the problem, explains Parker, the casino manager. The tribal-owned casinos on both the Fort Belknap and Rocky Boy's reservations struggle to attract gamblers from Havre, and the deck, so to speak, is stacked against them. At 20,000 square feet, Northern Winz Casino between Havre and Box Elder dwarfs any other gambling complex in the region and offers attractions like live music and 200 gaming machines, but there's little incentive for people to make short drive from Havre, where gaming machines are found throughout its bars and convenience stores. Montana's ten tribal casinos are given no advantage over any other gambling establishment in the state, like Class III games that would let players bet against each other. Free drinks are prohibited. At Northern Winz cashiers issue a W-2G form with any payout, which compels players to pay an average of 29% in taxes on their winnings. In Havre, says Parker, there is no such

Box Elder's Ah-Wah-Si-Sahk Skate Park on the Rocky Boy Reservation was built in 2018, a collaboration between the Chippewa Cree Tribe, Evergreen Skateparks, and Rock and Roll Hall of Famer Jeff Ament's foundation.

requirement. It begs the question, why would anyone drive out to Northern Winz if they can't keep all their winz?

Of course, it's unfair to paint all of Havre with a broad brush of racism. The Chamber of Commerce, for example, is taking steps to start changing some attitudes. Jody Olson, the Chamber's executive director, is committed to repairing the longstanding rift between the tribal members and Havre's business owners. At a time when Havre has seen the recent losses of Sears, Herbergers, and Kmart, as well as the shuttering of Amtrak's ticket office, the town needs that economic support more than ever. Shortly after starting her job with the Chamber in 2017, Olson made the unprecedented move of asking for some face time with the Tribal Council on Rocky Boy, so she could thank them directly for their economic contribution to the community. She also voiced her desire to develop a relationship between the tribe and the town that would be economically beneficial to both. "They said I was the first one (from Havre) to do that," she says. She invited all of Rocky Boy's 31 businesses to become members of the Havre Chamber, and a couple wound up enrolling within a few months of her visit.

Tribal member "Big" Mike Corcoran wasn't raised on Rocky Boy, but spent several summers there, visiting from Northern California where he was raised. He moved to the res to attend college in 2010 and never left. Although the six-foot-five, 390-pound ex-bouncer and occasional MMA fighter is seldom challenged directly by bigots (or anyone), he is keenly aware of the racial divide. "Out here, a lot of it comes from previous generations that are still around. People that have this hate that they were raised with, these stereotypes of natives out here, that we're all drunks, we're all thieves, you know. (They think) we're all on drugs, we're uneducated."

The racism and hatred emanating from Havre is being perpetrated by white people to their own detriment, he points out. Corcoran was part of a Rocky Boy Business Alliance study that found eight million dollars was spent by Rocky Boy residents in Havre over an eight-year period. "We're looking at about a million dollars a year just from our tribe, and there's another whole tribe at Fort Belknap, just on the other side of them. That kind of money rolls around the town about seven times. Somebody pays their employee, their employee goes to a restaurant and tips the waitress. That waitress goes and buys gas or a pack of smokes at the local convenience store, that type of thing. It's a symbiotic relationship."

Racism is as stubborn as a tick, but many feel there is hope. "Younger generations seem like they're not carrying over the hate, the discrimination," says the Havre shopkeeper. "There's only one way to erase racism and that's to raise your kids right." Upcoming generations are indeed more enlightened about racial identity, but people like Olson and Corcoran and other, progressive-minded Hi-Liners are not waiting around for racism to die off with older generations. They're actively working toward a future where tribal members and non-natives can coexist in an atmosphere of mutual respect.

In the summer of 2017 Corcoran saw a striking example of what could be. A wildfire broke out in the Bears Paw Mountains south of Beaver Creek Park, on the reservation. The Rocky Boy Agency Police Department headed up the response. "I went to the firefighters strategy meeting in the morning to take some pictures for the radio station," says Corcoran, who works at tribal station KHEW. "White people, native people, they're all standing side by side, ready to go fight these fires up in the mountains. Meanwhile, there are people on Facebook arguing over whether an Indian started the fire or a white person started the fire. Those people fighting the fire, they didn't give a damn what color the person was next to them. They didn't care anything about that. I thought that was great—I thought that would help bring us all together." He pauses, perhaps reflecting on the power of a common purpose. "There's a cultural difference, but we all want to put food on the table. We all want to keep the lights on; we all want to keep the water running at our houses. We all want to work so we can accomplish what we can for our families. We're all pretty much the same—people just don't realize it."

FINDING LOST LAKE

THE GOOD NEWS IS, LOST LAKE HAS BEEN FOUND.
One of Montana's most stunning geological odd-
ities is also one of its best-kept secrets, tucked
away in the gently rolling wheat fields of central
Montana near the Highwood Mountains between
Fort Benton and Great Falls. The site is so remote
that there's very little chance you've driven past it,
even by accident. Even many people who live in
the area are unaware of its existence. But it's worth
the effort, as you won't find a more breathtaking
natural formation in Russell Country. It's one of
those freaky Montana geological formations like
Medicine Rocks in the southeast or the stacked
boulders along Homestake Pass east of Butte, that
illustrate the endless variety of dramatic natural
features across the state. Once you've seen it, your
efforts to describe the Shonkin Sag and Lost Lake
will likely fail to do this incredible spot justice. Try
this: If Wyoming's Devils Tower was turned upside
down and used to punch a hole in the ground, the
hole would look something like Lost Lake. Situated at the terminus of Shonkin Sag, Lost Lake is
the remnant of a glacial river channel that once
featured a gushing wall of water twice the width
of Niagara Falls.

Lost Lake on the Shonkin Sag
was once the site of a waterfall
twice the size of Niagara Falls.

The Shonkin Sag, a massive fluvioglacial channel, begins in the Highwood Mountains and winds eastward through farm lands and ranches for a hundred miles or so, ending at the Judith River. At its widest point, the dry channel is two miles across, and reaches depths of 500 feet. A few glacial alkali lakes are still dotted across the bottom. *Roadside Geology of Montana* describes the Shonkin Sag as "one of the two or three most spectacular glacial melt water channels in the country."

The channel was formed during the last glacial period, between 13,000 and 17,000 years ago, although some scientists theorize that it is the result of repeated cycles. The massive expanse of water that's now the Missouri River had flowed northeastward from Glacial Lake Great Falls into an inland sea, or possibly the Hudson Bay. When ice sheets formed a blockage on the river, water and ice built up until it burst through the blockage and flowed out, carving a series of new channels. Once the lake retreated, water continued to flow along the Shonkin Sag channel at a much lower level, until it eventually dried up. It's been calculated that the waterfall that poured into Lost Lake during the Shonkin Sag's full flow would have been upwards of 300 feet tall, and a mile across.

Lost Lake, sometimes called Dry Falls, is a remnant of that channel. The bowl-shaped depression, several hundred feet deep and at least a half-mile wide, forms the eastern terminus of the Sag, and reveals the underlying geology that is prevalent in this area. It's known as a laccolith—an igneous intrusion between two sedimentary layers, resulting from volcanic activity 50 million years ago. The vertically striated shonkinite walls surrounding Lost Lake are reminiscent of the columnar basalt that forms the Devils Tower, and the 200-foot-thick walls run for a mile down the channel. The formation is quite dramatic, dropping straight away from the lip of the surrounding land some two hundred feet to vegetation-covered slopes that end at the edge of the opaque green water of the lake. The place has a prehistoric feel to it, like the ruins of a lost civilization in the midst of the Amazon jungle.

Towering laccolith formations are also grouped on the northern lip of the chasm, where it can be accessed by a nearby gravel road. The towers of rock have the appearance of lumps of squished modeling clay that were piled up and left to harden. Some rocks, as big as a Volkswagen Beetle, seem to have been sliced cleanly in half. Others have pockmarked caves and curves that appear to have been carved by a mad sculptor. With the ever-present wind whistling through the rock formations and the otherworldly appearance of the Lost Lake chasm, you can't help but be affected by this seemingly out-of-place freak of geology.

You'll pass a lot of cattle on the way there, but you'll also encounter lots of wildlife, from golden eagles and red-tailed hawks to pronghorns and white-tailed deer. The rock forest also seems to be a popular hangout for rabbits, perhaps providing quick shelter from cruising raptors above.

Getting there is tricky, but you can approach two ways: Drive in from County Road 80, which runs southeast out of Fort Benton, or take U.S. Route 87 east out of Great Falls and turn north on Highwood Road. Turn east on Shonkin Road and follow it around to Lost Lake Road. You may wind up driving right past the site more than once. It's not a state park or regional monument or anything that might provide an obvious marker. There's just a wide spot in the road where the rancher who owns the land allows parking. A small sign is there providing a warning to be careful, and a footpath leads through the sandy soil a few hundred yards to the rock formations. Bring a camera, because there's no way the folks back home are going to believe what you found in the middle of central Montana's farmland.

THE GUSTAFSONS, PILLARS OF CONRAD

I must have been shot in the rear end with luck when I was born.
From *ROOM TO ROAM* by "Rib" Gustafson, DVM

SITTING DOWN TO BREAKFAST WITH WYLIE GUSTAFSON at the Home Cafe in Conrad can be like trying to have a pint in a Dublin pub with Bono. From the moment he enters the front door, he's accosted by well-wishers and neighbors and old friends, and it's ten minutes before he can fold his angular frame into a booth. Wylie and the Wild West Show, his country and western band, are successful purveyors of traditional cowboy music, and their band is known worldwide. Wylie's a spectacular yodeler—that's his voice you hear on Yahoo!'s audio logo.

But it's not his fame as a musician that draws the attention here in his native Conrad. It's his bloodline.

"A prophet has no honor in his own country," he says with a wry smile as the server sets a Frisbee-sized pancake down in front of his three-year-old son, Orren. Wylie moved back to Conrad ten years ago from a ranch in eastern Washington, and it took five years for the locals to accept him as a serious rancher. "You've got to prove that you're nothing special." Wylie's known and liked, but it's his late father who is the indirect object of the affection. Conrad's first veterinarian, R. W. "Rib" Gustafson served the region for more than 20 years, from 1951 until his retirement in 1972. Rib and his family touched thousands of lives during that era, and his legacy still shines over Conrad like sun rays bursting through the clouds.

Wylie and his four older siblings—three brothers and a sister—had a unique upbringing in this fertile wedge of northern Montana known as the Golden Triangle.

The Gustafson Ranch spreads over 5,000 acres on the Two Medicine River on the Blackfeet Reservation.

Their dad was the only vet within a hundred-mile radius, and he was called out on emergencies constantly, sometimes in the middle of the night, already exhausted after a 16-hour day. But everybody in the Golden Triangle knew of "the Doc," and knew they could count on him when they needed help. The plucky vet would grab his medical bag and make the drive in his jacked-up, brown Chevy Impala (he never owned a truck), sometimes bringing a kid or two along to help out. Wylie recalls being pressed into service at the tender age of 12, helping his dad track down a pregnant heifer that was having trouble. "He'd put me behind the steering wheel, set me on his medicine box, and he'd get out on the front of the hood with his rope, and say just follow that cow, I don't care if it takes a half an hour. Pretty soon we'd get close enough where he could throw a loop over her, tie her to our bumper and do the operation. That's how I learned to drive."

Frequently the operation was a C-section, which Rib pioneered in the area. Until he began performing the calf-saving surgery, ranchers would typically have to euthanize a heifer that was in distress during calving.

Rib was a passionate doctor who employed a pragmatic approach but was adept at reassuring his clientele with a generous nature and quirky sense of humor. He was known to accept half a cow as payment if he was able to save it, and at one point he was owed 17 half-cows. He rarely collected on his debt. By the time his career was winding down in the seventies, someone suggested the gregarious raconteur should write a book to share all his experiences. *Under the Chinook Arch: Tales of a Montana Veterinarian* was published in 1993, and the brief, punchy chapters were packed with humor, affection, and sometimes hair-raising accounts of his life in animal medicine. His writing is direct, devoid of frills, and frequently uproarious, much like the man himself. A sequel, *Room to Roam,* was released in 1996, and Rib went on to write several more books. The first two books reveal a man who seemed to enjoy life to the fullest, had little patience for fools, and didn't see any reason to pull his punches about his true feelings. Chapter titles like "The Enema," "Pot Lickers" and "Milk Fever" offer the reader a clue that this isn't going to be your run-of-the-mill memoir.

"He would load (the books) up in the back of his car," says Erik "Fingers" Ray Gustafson, a teacher who, like his younger brother Wylie, learned to play the guitar by watching their dad. The two boys attended the University of Montana and, for a few years in the early eighties, played in the same band in Missoula. Meanwhile, Rib promoted his books. "He'd load up his brown Impala," says Erik, "and he would just take off on these toots where he would go into a bookstore or a restaurant, wherever people were, and he would give them a book and they'd go, 'Oh, thank you!' And he'd say, 'You're welcome, that'll be ten dollars.' He'd just go around and literally sell them out of the trunk of his car when he was in his seventies."

After retiring from his veterinary practice in Conrad, Rib and his wife Pat—who'd become an accomplished painter—sold the clinic and bought a 5,000-acre ranch near Browning, on the Two Medicine River. Rib raised a few cattle and took to breeding and training horses, specializing in rodeo and cutting horses. According to Wylie, Rib was the first to bring quarter horses into the Hi-Line. Also, he continued to provide medical attention to area livestock when needed.

Rib's eldest son Sid followed him into the veterinary field, and like his dad, is also a writer, having published a handful of novels and books on veterinary medicine. He lives in Bozeman. Daughter Kristen became an attorney and "did a lot of work for her worthless brothers," Wylie says. Son Barr, also a veterinarian, and his wife Colleen, a fifth-generation rancher, took over the family spread in 1970 and share their ranch house with several rambunctious dogs. A small sign above a kitchen cabinet reads "Horse work before housework."

"You don't make much money," Barr says, spreading some family photos out on the kitchen table, "but it's a lot of fun. We branded 270 calves this spring." Their son Owen rides rodeo in the summer and their daughter Greta is carrying on the family trade, working towards a DVM degree at Montana State.

The Gustafson clan grew outward from the ranch, but many relatives are still living and working in Conrad or up on the Hi-Line. "Our family's so extensive anymore," Rib wrote, "we can't say anything bad about anyone because we might be talking about a relative." Nowadays Rib Gustafson presides over the ranch from a ridge overlooking a cottonwood-filled oxbow in the Two Medicine River. He and his beloved wife Pat are represented by a pair of marble markers embedded in the prairie turf, their ashes scattered to the swirling winds that flow down from Canada, carrying the spirit and memory of one of Conrad's most beloved sons down along the Chinook Arch.

That lonesome old cowboy don't ride anymore.
He drifted away to a far distant shore.
But if you listen closely by the prairie's full moon,
You'll hear the wind whisper his heavenly tune.
From "THE COWBOY'S LULLABY" by Wylie Gustafson

SIPPING AND SINGING
ACROSS MONTANA

Montana may be one of the country's least populous states, but we're second only to Vermont in the number of craft breweries per capita. Big Sky Country is a thirsty place, and currently there are 82 craft breweries operating in Montana, with several in the works. Visiting all of the state's brewpubs sounds like a Herculean undertaking that would require several months, thousands of miles of travel, and maybe a spare liver. There's a Missoula man who's more than halfway there, but his primary mission is to entertain, not imbibe. Singer-songwriter John Floridis has played music in 59 Montana brewpubs, and he won't stop, he says, until he's played them all. Who better to provide a perspective on Montana's bounty of craft beers and its variety of tap houses in which to drink them?

Like many Montana troubadours who derive their living from playing music, Floridis is a road warrior. He's racked up more than 300,000 miles on his Honda Element bringing his music to the beer-sipping masses in brewpubs from HA Brewing Company in Eureka, just a stone's throw from Canada in the northwest, to Bandit Brewing in Darby, the southernmost brewery on Highway 93, and dozens of other breweries through the rest of the state. He's played tiny taprooms like Wildwood Brewing in Stevensville, to big, restaurant-sized operations like Tamarack Brewing in Lakeside in the Flathead Valley. He's nothing if not adaptable. "A lot of it is having the right gear," he says, "but it also tests you as a musician," he says of the wide variety of taprooms—and crowds—he plays for. "You make it a challenge. You can't say, 'Oh, I'm a virtuoso musician and I'm going to obliterate everybody with my virtuosity.' Bring

that energy into the room but check in on how people are reacting because it is still a human interaction, and you're seeing how the music is engaging people at any given place."

Onstage, he employs an intricate rig of looping devices and effects pedals to create a sound that can rival that of a full band. Or, when the situation calls for it, he'll gently finger-pick a delicate instrumental on his acoustic guitar.

Some brewpubs, he says, are rowdy and raucous, and it's harder to tell if his efforts are getting through. He recalls a show he performed in Great Falls at a brewery called The Front. "The din was pretty strong in that room. The victory, I think, came in an odd way. It's packed, it's loud, so I'm not just playing 'Fire and Rain' to myself. It's not sensitive music." Despite his aggressive attack, he wasn't getting so much as a second glance from anyone in the crowded room. "I don't know if it's a Great Falls thing—they are lovely people in Great Falls. I don't need to be the center of attention, but give me some acknowledgment. I need to be recognized as a living, breathing thing. I was getting nothing. So I get done and go to the bar to get a beer, and the manager says, 'Oh my god, they love you. They think you're fantastic, we're getting so many compliments. Come back any time.' So I had to wrap my head around that. This was the reality."

Floridis concedes that he has been pretty light on covering the breweries of eastern Montana, like Beaver Creek Brewery in Wibaux, Meadowlark Brewing in Sidney or Busted Knuckle Brewery in Glasgow. That's mostly due to the reality of the troubadour's lifestyle, especially when they're playing the breweries. Typically, the taprooms will feature two hours of music, usually in the early evening, and the pay scale is all over the map. Some breweries will pay a musician $200 or more for a night, where others supply only a tip jar. Either way, it's a tough nut to crack for a musician to drive up to 600 miles each way and come home with anything to show for their efforts. For that reason, says Floridis, he'll try to string together consecutive nights of shows if there's a good amount of traveling. "You gotta try to make it fit into a routing that makes some kind of (financial) sense. There are some of the farther flung ones I haven't hit. Most of them are on the east side." He's determined to mark them all off his list, although there are new breweries popping up every year. "It's like Whack-a-Mole now. It's hard to keep up with them all," he says with a laugh.

A successful brewpub musician must also be adept at reading the crowd and trying to entertain them in a way that doesn't ruffle too many feathers. Travis Yost, a Missoula musician who frequently teams up with Floridis (and has embarked on his own brewery tour), tells of playing a Prince song before a crowd of conservatives in Libby, about a half hour from the Idaho panhandle in the northeast. It didn't go over too well with that particular bunch, and one patron even shouted a homophobic slur at him. Floridis, who plays mostly original compositions, had a different, wholly unexpected experience in the same brewpub. "I hadn't been to Libby in a long time," he says. "I come into town, and there's a big confederate flag on display in front of this business, and I'm thinking, 'Oh, god, what have I done?' and like this beacon of light coming through the cloud, there's Cabinet Mountain Brewing, this wonderful little nirvana of all these people, they're all getting along, and they're drinking craft beer. And it's run entirely by women." Like the vast majority of his Montana taproom gigs, the brewery staff treated him great and the gig went just fine.

Similarly, when he found himself surrounded by loud conversations about guns and ammunition a few years ago at a taproom in Laurel, near Billings, it was a reminder that his home base of Missoula is a progressive island surrounded by a big, conservative state. "But the beer was flowing and it was out on the porch," he says of the Laurel gig. "It was a good vibe. Dipping into a different culture is a good thing. It's more about finding these moments of connection, of finding things in common. I think that the stuff I do, musically and in general just the kind of energy I put into a room can be universal."

While Montana's six regions display a real contrast to each other in style and substance, one place where nearly everyone can get together is over some cold glasses of great homegrown beer and some Montana-bred music to provide the soundtrack. John Floridis is doing his part to make sure every brewery in the state will eventually have the chance to share his particular brand of rhythm and brews.

An old Jeep pickup laden with fresh cut firewood sits outside a restaurant on Main Street in Philipsburg. Photo © Jonathan Qualben

GOLD WEST COUNTRY

THE PRECIOUS METAL THAT INSPIRED the real westward expansion is a fitting name for the southwest corner of Montana, although it's copper, not gold, that gilds the heart of Gold West Country. Butte, home of the Copper Kings, might just top the list of the state's most interesting towns, with its multi-cultural history and bare-knuckle reputation. Butte natives tend to be born with a chip on their shoulder, but you'll never find anyone more loyal. Our mining history radiates across the Gold West region out of Butte, to places like Virginia City and its shocking Vigilante legend, and a whole network of ghost towns from Bannack to Garnet. During Butte's heyday, nearby Anaconda was its smelter town, and the "Anaconda Stack," the world's tallest brick structure, still stands as a testament to the area's rich mining past.

Other, darker chapters of Western history can be explored on the Big Hole River, at the Nez Perce National Historical Park. Like the nearby Big Hole National Battlefield, it's a sobering reminder that America's history, especially in the West, is not nearly as egalitarian and benevolent as we've sometimes been led to believe.

Music buffs will find plenty to celebrate in southwest Montana. Butte has established one of the Northwest's biggest music weekends with the Montana Folk Festival, which grew out of the National Folk Festival that was held there from 2008 to 2010. If you'd rather play a little air guitar and rock out, there's Rockin' the Rivers, just down I-90 near Cardwell. This three-day rock blowout has featured classic rockers like Journey and Head East to more head-banging acts like Skid Row and Queensrÿche. Red Ants Pants Festival in White Sulphur Springs offers an eclectic lineup of A-list roots artists from Ruby Boots to Dwight Yoakam.

Quieter outdoor pursuits abound throughout Gold West Country, too. The Continental Divide runs right down the spine of the region, from the spectacular Scapegoat Wilderness down through the Anaconda Range. National Forests offer almost limitless recreation opportunities from snowmobiling and skiing in the winter to fishing, hiking and camping in the summer. I know people camp in the winter too, but that's just crazy.

Visitors traveling between the two National Parks have ample opportunity to check out the treasures of Gold West Country on their journey any time of year. Helena, the state capital, located halfway between Yellowstone and Glacier, has its own gold-rush past, memorialized with places like the Last Chance Gulch walking mall, built on the very spot that produced $19 million worth of gold in its first four years. Helena also offers a terrific museum, tours of the Capitol, first-rate theatre, live music, great microbrews, and some of the friendliest people you'll find in a Montana city. If you do visit, try to resist using the old "in a handbasket" joke. They've heard it.

A familiar landmark in the Flint
Valley between Philipsburg and
Drummond is this pair of trees in
Hall, sporting dozens of skulls.

Kevin Owens and Chris Cerquone of
Missoula push a sled full of gear out
onto Georgetown Lake, where they'll
drill through 30 inches of ice to fish.

"Hill and Valley," Steven Siegel's house-sized art structure at
Blackfoot Pathways: Sculpture in the Wild near Lincoln.

IF YOU'RE GAME,
THEY HAVE THE GAME

THEY CAME FOR THE GOLD. THEY STAYED for the meat. That might be a gross oversimplification, but every autumn in Ennis, a hundred years after the gold ran out, they do bring the meat. Located near Yellowstone National Park in the Madison Valley, Ennis is a former gold rush town, now a ranch community with a fly fishing problem. That is to say, its proximity to Montana's world-class trout streams makes it a fly fishing nerve center that supports half a dozen shops and a handful of outfitters in the summer. Many of its 850 residents are also hunters, and the annual Hunters Feed is a block party that serves up a smorgasbord of wild game-based dishes that run the gamut from the prosaic to the sublime. It's become one of Ennis's most anticipated events. There's a competitive element, with awards and prizes going to the recipes that receive the most votes from the public. For 34 years the annual ritual has kicked off hunting season by giving everyone a chance to empty their freezers of last year's bounty, bringing Ennis together for a street party in the process.

The trout-filled Madison River runs past Ennis out of West Yellowstone, and most travelers on State Highway 87 cruise right through on their way to or from the National Park. But for those who take the time to hang out for a while, they discover that Ennis, like most of Montana's small towns, has a personality and feel all its own. The population quadruples in the months with no "R" as snowbirds flock here to spend the warmer months. Many of them have already fled for parts south when the Hunters Feed happens in October.

"There's people here (in the winter)," says Karen Frey-Suplee, year-round resident, "but it's a little more chill." It's unclear if she means that literally as she plops one of her "elk-alope" meatballs called *Frikkadellen* into a tiny Dixie cup for a Hunters Feed patron. As she carefully tops it with a spoonful of "fire gravy," she says how she loves eating elk, and grew up with this traditional German dish. "It's the original hamburger. The elk gives it a nice bottom. Elk is like the best free-range beef I ever had." The elk-antelope blend has a strong flavor but doesn't seem to have much of that off-putting gaminess not present in a nice, plastic-wrapped package of store-bought hamburger. The fire gravy helps.

As tasty as the *Frikkadellen* is, elk is pretty ho-hum compared with other meats found at a typical Hunters Feed. A recent edition of the event featured 18 entries,

"Madison Valley Angler," by Belgrade artist Jim Dolan, greets visitors to Ennis in the Madison Valley.

including stews and chili containing more uncommon game like bear, caribou, moose, and mountain sheep. While stews and chilis were well-represented, there were many less traditional vehicles for the meats, like spring rolls and *queso* dip. One clever participant even whipped up a sugary treat called "Sweet Wild Thangs," candied pecan pralines dipped in caramel containing finely ground elk meat.

Grinding seemed to be the go-to method of preparation. Some meats, like the bear used in something called "Boo Boo Biscuits & Gravy," were mixed with a blend of spices and ground pork sausage. It was quite tasty, and the grinding mitigated the base texture of bear meat, which can be stringy and greasy like an overcooked rump roast.

The cooks tend to be cagey when it comes to disclosing specifics about their recipes, guarding them like a fisherman protecting his favorite trout hole. Matt Sheffield, whose "Sheffield's Pie" won the top prize at this particular Hunters Feed, enthusiastically promotes his mixture of antelope and mountain sheep, which is topped with a dollop of tangy mashed potato and parsnip mix. "The antelope is less gamey, and it's refreshing," he says, tickling the air with his fingertips. "But it still has the integrity of the flavor." When asked what spices are used, he mumbles something about some parsnip in the meat, but then clams up. After all, this is head-to-head competition with twenty of his neighbors. A year's worth of bragging rights are at stake. After a few moments of consideration, he declines to name even a single spice, reacting indignantly, as if he's been asked to spill the combination to the safe containing the family jewels. "I'm not going to give you my recipe," he says flatly.

Halley Perry, an energetic, thirty-something brunette with a quick smile and an indefatigable drive, is the executive director of Ennis's Chamber of Commerce. That means she's the boss of Hunters Feed. After the event is over, the winners have been announced, and the crowd has moved down the street to the critter call competition at the distillery, she kicks back behind her desk in the Chamber office and waves away a suggestion that the afternoon's mayhem must be exhausting. "Fourth of July is the big one. Ten thousand people are in the streets for the Fourth." She describes a shoulder-to-shoulder mob filled with tourists from all over, swelling the little town to a sweaty mob at the peak of summer. Hunters Feed, conversely, is pretty much locals only. The scene bears her out: most vehicles parked downtown bear Madison County plates, and every fourth or fifth vehicle is mud-splattered ATV. There are lots of camo and Filson vests, and cowboy hats are worn non-ironically. It's mostly the locals of Madison County, gathering on Ennis's three-block main street to reconnect with old friends, chow down and vote on a wide sampling of tasty game dishes, and share the excitement of the new hunting season. It's a truly communal event with plenty of room for local clubs who set up booths and sell raffle ticket for a hunting rifle or high-end cooler, or, like the Lions Club ladies at a table fronting the sidewalk, hawking a cookbook featuring game recipes.

And for those of us who never became accustomed to the primal funk of wild game? Hunters Feed will be just fine without us—it just means more meat for them.

A CREEPY LOOK AT LIFE BEHIND BARS

IN THE HEART OF GOLD WEST COUNTRY lies a sort of Bermuda Triangle nestled in the rolling hills just east of the Continental Divide. There's the state mental hospital in Warm Springs, the state prison near Deer Lodge, and the country's largest Superfund site in Butte, all situated within 41 miles of each other. Is there some unseen connection between a mental hospital, a penitentiary, and a whole town known for its mile-long pond laden with arsenic, heavy metals, and deadly carcinogens? It makes one wonder.

Butte's rough-and-tumble history is well-documented in the venerable mining town, with several museums and historic markers celebrating 150 years of digging up the Richest Hill on Earth. Up the freeway at Warm Springs, Montana's state psychiatric facility has no museums per se, but the hospital, which was established even before Montana became a state, holds its share of grim history, including a secret program that forcibly sterilized 256 people over a 30-year period.

And then there's Deer Lodge. Opened in 1979, the Montana State Prison houses some 1,500 inmates in a mountain valley about three miles west of town. Before that, Montana's miscreants and lawbreakers were incarcerated in the foreboding, almost medieval behemoth known today as the Old Montana Prison. The twenty-foot high rock wall surrounding a massive complex of cell blocks still stands in the middle of Deer Lodge as a striking beacon to Montana's past. It was opened as the territorial prison in 1871, when its first nine prisoners were led through the iron gates. What could life have been like for a convict in those days? You can see for yourself on one of the tours that wind through the old prison. Tag along with one of the Museum's knowledgeable tour guides, or you can wander the expansive prison grounds on a self-guided mosey.

Better yet, sign up for the Halloween midnight ghost tour. If you've got the guts.

The popular tour is an annual event that quickly fills up with paranormal investigators, thrill-seeking history buffs, and people who just want to test the limits of their bravado. You'll be allowed to check out areas of the prison that are off-limits to daytime tours, and visitors can learn about some of the most savage examples of man's inhumanity to man that eventually led to prison reform. To ensure that everyone's imaginations are rolling at full boil, museum staff break out the "special" photos, gory black and white glossies of some of the

At the Deer Lodge Old Prison Museum, the damage from a riot-quelling bazooka round is plainly visible on the tower where two of the ringleaders were holed up in the 1959 melee.

most brutal beatings, stabbings, slashings and head bashings perpetrated by prisoners and guards alike during the prison's long and violent history. Tours are $50 a pop, and typically run from 9:30 PM to 2:30 AM and beyond. It is most definitely not for those with a delicate constitution. A museum employee, usually outfitted in vintage prison stripes, begins the tour in the museum gift shop. Participants can pore over the aforementioned crime scene photos or watch a video presentation of the prison's history while the paranormal crowd double-checks the batteries in their EVP recorders, tests the levels on their REM-pods and futz with other ghost-tracking gizmos before heading out.

The first stop is the burned-out prison theater, which houses the "galloping gallows." The stark hangman's structure features thirteen wooden steps that lead to the last place many Montana felons would ever stand. While only two prisoners were executed within these prison walls, the contraption was hauled all over the state to perform hangings, hence the moniker. It bears mentioning that there is no heat or electricity in the old prison, and the cold darkness ratchets up the level of creepiness.

From the gallows the tour moves back outdoors past a raised concrete foundation, all that's left of the original cell block, built in 1870. The tour guide describes the overcrowding and primitive living conditions the prisoners had to endure until new cell blocks were completed. Oh, and by the way, at this point the tour group is standing directly atop the original prison cemetery. Only 25 of the 27 bodies interred in the graveyard were found when it was relocated. The tour takes an even darker turn as it approaches the administration building. A set of concrete steps leads down to the doorway to the Hole, a seven-foot square cell where the worst of the worst were locked away in sweltering isolation. Its location next to the boiler room kept the concrete bunker's temperature in the nineties. Authorities put the kibosh on the Hole after an inmate's heart exploded in 1967 on Halloween night. His internal organs were reportedly 40 degrees higher than normal, even hours after his death.

Once inside the admin building's main office, the explorers gather in the darkness, their shadows dancing on the walls as flashlights and cell phones provide jumpy illumination. Some more history is shared by the tour guide, much of it about Frank Conley, the most beloved—and hated—of the wardens who served over the course of the prison's century of use. During Conley's three decades as warden, he oversaw several building projects including a theater and a wood shop that expanded the capacity of the prison and enhanced the lives of its inmates. He also put inmates to work in the 1890s building the prison's formidable wall, including the six crenellated guard towers that give it the look of an ancient castle. Under Conley's ambitious reign, prisoners also built and ran a brickyard and a lumber mill and grew their own food. Conley's army of convict laborers constructed eleven buildings for the Montana State Hospital at Warm Springs, four buildings for the Montana State Tuberculosis Sanitorium in Galen, and hundreds of miles of state roads. Conley believed that a convict working on a crew away from the prison "awakens to a new appreciation of life and determines to make a better future." The warden began rubbing elbows with Copper King William A. Clark and other political bigwigs, using prison-grown food to supply parties he held at his lavish house across the street, which he'd had built to his specifications. Eventually, a governor's investigation into Conley's wanton use of state resources, i.e., prison labor, to support his cushy lifestyle resulted in the warden being sacked from his position. He immediately took over as mayor of Deer Lodge, where he continued to wield his influence until his death in 1939. Whether Conley's ghost haunts the inner sanctum of the admin building is up for debate, but his legacy, in the form of the Old Montana Prison's collection of imposing brick buildings, is undeniable. Over the century of the prison's existence, multiple escape attempts were foiled, one of which left Conley with a slash from a convict's blade that required 103 stitches. Several prison riots were quelled, the most famous being the 1959 melee that held the town of Deer Lodge in a grip of terror until the National Guard fired a round from a WWII-era bazooka into a tower where two instigators, Jerry Myles and Lee Smart, were holed up. The huge divot taken out by the bazooka round is plainly visible near the top of the brick tower on Cellblock 1, the only lasting evidence of the prison's bloodiest riot. The midnight ghost tour allows those brave enough to climb the stairs and enter the room where the dramatic murder-suicide of Myles and Smart ended the 36-hour siege. According to the museum staff, several visitors have reported seeing the two doomed convicts in the room, or hearing conversations between them. For those who can muster the courage to visit the death room at the top of the tower, the trip down the stairs is usually much quicker than the trip up.

The Old Museum Prison Complex is a great way to spend half a day in Deer Lodge, about an hour's drive from Missoula. The prison itself is an eye-opening look at the depressing conditions that were acceptable for convicted felons during Montana's first century.

ALMOST THE TRUMPETER SWAN SONG

IN MANY WAYS, 1932 WAS AN UGLY YEAR IN THE UNITED STATES. The Dow Jones bottomed out at 41.22 points, its lowest level of the Great Depression. The Lindbergh baby was kidnapped and found dead ten weeks later near the family home in New Jersey. And just when we could really use a drink, the repeal of prohibition was still more than a year away. But there was a glimmer of hope—the magnificent trumpeter swan, which was widely believed to have gone extinct, was found, thriving at the warm springs of Red Rock Lakes in south central Montana.

By the 1930s, the native species in the contiguous U.S. was pretty close to winking out forever, with only about 70 birds remaining south of Canada, most of which were found at Red Rock Lakes. Several factors had combined to nearly seal the graceful

Trumpeter swans were thought to be headed for extinction until a small population was found in the 1930s on Red Rocks Lake near the Centennial Mountains. Photo © Jonathan Qualben

swan's doom. Its long feathers had been over harvested to provide decoration for women's fashionable hats, and they also were in demand for use as writing quills. Similar fashion trends had also led to the aggressive predation of beavers and muskrat, animals that build the mounds on which the trumpeter swans made their nests. Fortunately, President Franklin D. Roosevelt (who'd defeated a Depression-tainted Hoover the same year the swans were discovered to be not quite extinct) signed an executive order in 1935 that established the Red Rock Lakes National Wildlife Refuge, providing a protected habitat for the trumpeter swan just in the nick of time.

North Americas largest waterfowl, trumpeters can weigh as much as 30 pounds and have a wingspan of eight feet, almost twice the size of the nearly-identical tundra swan. The birds are so heavy they can need as much as one hundred yards of "run-way" when they take off. Their distinctive trumpeting call is a thrilling sound to hear, especially as a flock passes overhead. They also honk it up quite a bit during mating and egg-laying season. Trumpeters typically choose a lifelong mate, and the mating display includes slow, synchronized swimming, lots of bill dipping and blowing air into the water. After mating, the pair will build a nest, typically a mound constructed atop a beaver lodge or manmade platform. They pile sedges and cattail tubers on the nest until it's about a foot and a half above the water. In early May the female, called a pen, lays anywhere from three to nine eggs. The male, or cob, raises a pretty good racket during the laying, trumpeting like a proud papa handing out cigars in the maternity ward waiting room. The pen incubates the eggs for five weeks, sometimes covering them with grass so she can go forage for food. In June the cygnets hatch and are usually paddling around in the water within a couple days. Early on they feed on insects and tiny crustaceans, sometimes dabbling the critters up from the bottom of the pond. They molt at about four to six weeks, acquiring gray plumage and a mottled black pattern on their bills. The parents also molt at that time, but interestingly, not simultaneously. Molting renders the swan incapable of flight, so only one parent molts at a time, making sure one of them can always fly while raising cygnets. The young ones learn to fly before ice appears on the pond. By their second year, the juveniles have attained their full adult plumage.

Located in the Centennial Valley within the Greater Yellowstone ecosystem, Red Rock Lakes National Wildlife Refuge is among the highest in the continental U.S., ranging from 6,600 feet to almost 10,000 feet in altitude. The area is also home to moose, bears, pronghorn, wolves, and dozens of other mammals. Trumpeter swans share the skies and nesting grounds with several other large avian species such as eagles, hawks and falcons. Migratory birds such as the sandhill crane can also be seen in the refuge, along with dozens of grassland species and waterfowl. It's a spectacular place for birdwatching, and one of the few areas in the lower 48 where you can see the trumpeter swan in a natural setting. It's pretty remote, though, and getting there requires driving almost 30 miles on a tire-popping rough dirt road. It can be more than a hundred miles round trip from the nearest gas station, so be prepared.

The main reason the swans congregate here is the warm spring that pumps into Red Rock Lakes year-round. The trumpeter's diet consists almost exclusively of aquatic herbage such as water weed, pondweed, water milfoil, and duck potato. They need open water to be able to feed, which they do by dabbling—upending themselves and rooting around with their bills, stirring up plants from the bottom. An adult male will consume as much as twenty pounds of vegetation in a day. They're a notoriously shy bird, highly sensitive to human activity. Development near their nesting grounds, such as summer homes and summertime water recreation, can cause the trumpeter swans to abandon their nest, even leave their eggs behind. Although the population has rebounded, human encroachment and development has destroyed much of the trumpeter swans' habitat, typically non-freezeover riparian areas with moving water and low-lying mounds they use for nesting. If they abandon their nest, it's difficult for them to find a new site that hasn't already been claimed by other trumpeters.

From that Depression-era low of 70, the population of trumpeters at Red Rock alone has leveled off at about 450 permanent residents. When migratory birds come down from larger herds in Canada and Alaska, the population swells to as much as 4,500. In the early 1960s the U.S. Fish and Wildlife Service biologists became concerned that the overcrowding might lead to the spread of disease and lack of available food source, so wildlife managers began relocating them to areas where the necessary resources were previously abundant, like Turnbull NWR in Washington and Lacreek NWR in South Dakota. Thanks to these efforts, the trumpeter swan can be seen on all four of the major North American flyways: the Pacific, Central, Mississippi and Atlantic.

While virtually every area of Montana struggles with the ongoing wrestling match of wildlife protection versus our use of natural resources, we can mark a solid "win" in the wildlife column here in Gold West Country. Red Rock Lakes National Wildlife Refuge, with its isolated location and warm spring, remains a stronghold for the trumpeter swan, a conservation success story. Thanks to the timely stroke of a pen by FDR, this remarkable creature has repopulated its habitats in North America and remains one of the most exciting subjects of observation for birders and wildlife enthusiasts willing to put in some bumpy miles to get to Red Rock Lakes.

CHEESEBURGER IN PARADISE

MONTANA HAS A PRETTY GOOD VARIETY of killer hamburgers. The Ugly Burger, served by Rod's Drive Inn in Havre, is known far and wide as big, messy and satisfying. In Missoula, many go to the Missoula Club, a downtown blue-collar bar, for its austere but incomparable Mo Burger. Burger Bob's in Bozeman is a tasty load, featuring a full half-pound of ground sirloin. If you find yourself traveling through the Blackfeet Reservation, you can swing in to The Nations Burger Station in Browning, where the burgers are served on native frybread.

Obviously, you can stack lots of highway miles chasing down the state's most memorable hamburgers. Or you could just point your ride to Drummond, about 45 minutes east of Missoula, where Parker's Family Restaurant offers quality and quantity with a hamburger menu so long it requires a three-ring binder. Budget some time to peruse the list, because there are 136 variations (as of this writing) on the American classic.

From the standard bacon cheeseburger, the menu quickly veers off into the indulgent and tantalizing to the downright bizarre. For example, there's the Bolster Burger: "Loaded burger topped with fries, a grilled cheese sandwich, and another ¼-lb. burger patty with American cheese." That's right, a hamburger topped with another lunch.

Jennifer Parker puts the finishing touches on the daily specials at Parker's Family Restaurant in Drummond, where the menu features 136 different hamburgers.

McDonald's Value Menu, this is not. So how did the exotic burger collection get started, and how did it spin so far out of control?

Just before opening time on a late October morning, co-owner Jennifer Parker is up on her knees in a booth, using a marker to draw cartoons on a whiteboard laid on the table. "This is my 'me' time in the morning, when people leave me alone," she laughs. She's an adroit cartoonist, and the fat-cheeked chefs and mustachioed cowboys she draws next to the list of today's specials provide a bit of a clue that it's all about having fun.

Before moving to their present location at 32 East Front Street, Jennifer and her husband Brent leased the local Frosty Freeze for about a year and half. "He was running burger specials every day. We kept track of them, and I'd save pictures of them. We had about 50 burgers when we bought this place. I said to Brent, what do we want to serve at this place? 'Uh, how about hamburgers?' It just kind of went from there."

There is one person she knows of who has had each of the 136 hamburgers on the menu, a local guy named Shannon Wortman. "That was before the menu was revised," she adds, explaining that at least a dozen burgers have since been added, perhaps providing a subtle challenge to Mr. Wortman, who smiles down from a photo on the wall behind the cash register.

Another reason that the hamburgers are so consistently good is that Brent is no mere line cook. He's a trained chef, having been classically trained in French cuisine at the California Culinary Institute in San Francisco. Occasionally one of the dinner specials, like frogs legs or escargot or a rabbit stew called *Lapin a la Chausseur*, will hint at his culinary skills. "He proposed to me with cheesecake," says Jennifer, her expression softening. "It was fabulous. His Alfredo sauce is to die for." The restaurant periodically hosts an evening of wine-paired meals, where Brent really gets to flex his gastronomic muscle, but it's the hamburgers that keep the customers streaming through the door.

Check out this gut-buster that will satisfy even the most ravenous appetite. It's called the Monster in Law: "A cross between a monster and a mother in law, this burger starts with crispy tots then a ½ lb. patty topped with ham, pepperoni, swiss and American cheese, chili cheese Fritos and curly fries, sour cream, jalapenos, and black olives."

While the no-calories-barred burger creations might make a cardiologist reach for his defibrillator, the Parkers pride themselves on using only the best quality ingredients for their menu. "We had to fire Sysco (a restaurant food supplier) in our first year because they couldn't guarantee us Montana beef," says Jennifer, shaking her head in dismay. "Our neighbors raise cows!" Local beef seems like a legit requirement in Drummond, self-proclaimed home of "World Class Bull Shippers." Parker's double-grinds their beef in-house, and they also hand-cut their fries and bake their own buns. And don't expect burger joint-type speed. Chain restaurants might be able to crank out an order in under three minutes, but as Brent explains, each order at

Parker's constitutes individual treatment in the kitchen. And some of these complicated burgers take a while to construct. When asked which of the hamburgers is his favorite to prepare, Brent demurs, but does allow, "There are probably ones I enjoy making less. And when you're back in the kitchen and there's 30 or 40 burgers on the wheel, it gets crazy." He gets plenty of help from their son Brent II, who graduated from Missoula's Culinary College.

Brent also teaches cooking to local high school kids, which he loves. "And the kids love him," says Jennifer. "He keeps them movin' and groovin'." While she doesn't get involved in the kitchen ("I can cook, I just hate to"), her effusive, wise-cracking personality is perfect for front-of-house. She also provided the restaurant's decor, which features hundreds of vintage Coca-Cola bottles, glasses, signs and polar bears. "A lot of this comes from my garage sale stash," she says.

Here's a selection that's guaranteed to feed your cheeseburger jones. This poetically simple burger with a diabolical twist is called the Silverback: "½-pound loaded cheeseburger topped with a ¼-pound loaded cheeseburger."

For customers with enough patience to leaf through the entire burger menu, especially if you're a movie buff, some delights await. "The Big Kahuna," "The Royale with Cheese," and the recently added "Five Dollar Milkshake" are all inspired by memorable scenes in *Pulp Fiction*. There are also "Big Fat Greek Burger" (greens, sun-dried tomatoes, black olives, pepperoncini and feta cheese), "The Blues Brothers Burger" (crumbled Gorgonzola, bacon, Swiss cheese, shredded lettuce and tomato), and the multi-meat salvo called "Mr. Holland's Opus" (double burger with ham, bacon, sausage and cheese). Jennifer claims to have 250 more burger ideas on her computer, and Brent II frequently dreams up new ideas. They've even added several creations that were suggested by their regulars. "One day Buck Buchanan walks in and screams, 'Brent, make me a plain hamburger with no bullsh*t!' So, now we offer 'Buck's No Bullsh*t Burger,' a quarter-pound patty on a bun with nothing else."

Although Parker's is right off I-90 just a few miles from the heavily-traveled Garrison Junction turnoff between Helena and Missoula, Jennifer says 83 percent of their business comes from local customers. Parker's is a Drummond gathering place where people come to share gossip, and sometimes just to get a gander at the latest additions to the burgeoning burger menu. With so many choices, and so many customers passing through from all over the place, it must be hard to pin down the hamburger that's ordered most often. "The bacon cheeseburger," Jennifer says without hesitation. "It's the first one on the menu! Can you believe it?"

YOUR NEXT BEST DRIVE

Digging deep into Montana, all 147,040 square miles of it, requires a lot of road work. Especially when you get out in the eastern plains, everything is just so far apart. Researching this book involved a ton of driving. Also, a lot of camping, some rubber tramping (sleeping in the car), a handful of motels, and a few friends' guest rooms. During a seven month period of travel I listened to two audio books, dozens of podcasts, and thousands of songs. Three different vehicles carried me across Montana, and according to the wacky spider-web of pink highlighter lines tracing routes across my battered and taped Montana highway map, I logged more than 4,000 miles. I've driven roads of all kinds, from fast and smooth interstates to two-lane blacktop state highways, from gravel county roads all the way down to muddy two-tracks that led me off the main drag to some obscure but fascinating destination.

Every road in Montana takes on a different personality in different seasons, and a few drives stand out in my mind as particularly memorable—singular journeys that, for one reason or another, are worth mentioning.

One mile long and 1,780 feet deep, the Berkeley Pit in Butte can be viewed from an overlook on the south end. Currently a water treatment system is being installed that will remove toxins such as arsenic, cadmium, and zinc before the water is released into Silver Bow Creek.

Whether you're a longtime Montanan who recognizes every one of these drives, or a newcomer or visitor who might want to seek them out when you're nearby, there's a pretty good chance you'll have your own memorable experience behind the wheel.

The Beartooth Highway is a no-brainer, and it's possibly the biggest source of hyperbolic adjectives in this book. If you're traveling to or from Yellowstone National Park, it's worth building an extra day into your visit to take this stunning drive between Red Lodge and Cooke City, near Yellowstone's northeast entrance. It's impassable in the winter, but when springtime hits and a 15-foot tall channel is plowed to allow traffic, it's worth the wait. I've driven it twice, and both times I encountered a couple of friendly herds of mountain goats near the summit.

Out in southeast Montana, State Route 39 runs north from Lame Deer on the Cheyenne Reservation through Colstrip and up to I-90 just west of Forsythe. It's a two-lane road with a great variety of scenery. The fifty-mile stretch goes from open plains into low, rolling hills, then the kinks in the road tighten as it bends through the pine-studded sandstone outcroppings that cover much of this pocket of the state. As you near Colstrip you will likely see a ton of wildlife, which are attracted to the rich vegetation growing on the reclaimed areas around the Rosebud coal mine. It feels like a little piece of western Montana out in the east.

Another favorite drive, which I got to make several times, is the postcard-pretty stretch of U.S. Route 2 that wraps around the southern end of Glacier National Park. This is the longest highway in Montana, at 667 miles, running border to border. It includes the Hi-Line, which couldn't be much different than this section that hugs the serpentine Middle Fork of the Flathead River between West Glacier and East Glacier. You're looking into Glacier Park directly across the river, and the state has wisely provided numerous turnouts where you can pull over and get some photos of Mount Nicholas and other rugged peaks that poke into the clouds. It can be slow going in the winter, but many of us make it slow going in the summer too. It's a main business thoroughfare between East Glacier and West Glacier, but why would you want to rush through all this gorgeous scenery?

The Lewis and Clark Highway between Townsend and Forsyth—otherwise known as U.S. Route 12—is the epitome of the "blue highway" that calls for adventurous travelers to disengage the cruise control. Heading west, it moseys through bucolic farmland from the middle of Custer Country, across the southern end of Russell Country, into the mountain ranges of Gold West Country. Along these 442 miles you'll drive alongside knobby basalt and gneiss rimrock, lined up like city skylines. Mountain ranges like the Bulls and Castles stand far apart, as if taking advantage of all the elbow room. You'll pass through small ranching and farming communities like Harlowton, Roundup, the curiously infamous Two Dot, and little Ingomar, home of the legendary Jersey Lilly. The people who make their lives here are as much a part of the landscape as the land they work. They work in oil and gas exploration, they raise cattle, they grow hay and alfalfa, and many of them have never traveled as far as Missoula or Billings their entire lives. And they're fine with that. Spend some time along Highway 12 and you'll get to know the real Montana.

Perhaps my favorite thing I've come across while traversing the state is a safety feature. Most of us are familiar with the rumble strip—the series of indentations stamped along the outer edge of the asphalt that create a loud, jarring vibration when your vehicle drifts across them. Starting in 2015, the state DOT began a five-year project to install rumble strips down the centerlines of state two-lane roads. I know many vehicles now offer things like lane-change alarms, proximity alerts, automatic braking and everything but fresh espresso. But I can tell you from experience that this $5,000-a-mile highway project is a most effective and welcome feature. More than once, I'll admit, I've been momentarily distracted and my car drifted across that centerline. The shock of the sudden, loud buzz from that rumble strip got my attention quicker than a flashing blue light in the rearview.

The potential perils of travel bring me to my next stretch of road which has always been one of my favorites but now carries the memory of a close brush with death. A couple of miles after westbound I-90 passes St. Regis west of Missoula, the freeway begins a series of graceful curves that wind through a canyon along the St. Regis River in the Lolo National Forest. I was driving along this stretch in mid-December of 2017, en route to pick up my daughter in Spokane for Christmas break. The blacktop looked deceptively bare, but I was going too fast for the snowy conditions. I found out later that this particular curve in the freeway was notorious for black ice. It's in the shade much of the day, not giving ice a chance to melt. I hit an invisible patch of ice

A cyclist rides in the Ovando Gran Fondo, an annual 55-mile bike tour through some of western Montana's most scenic landscape.
Photo © Jonathan Qualben

and slid off the right shoulder doing about 70 mph. My 4Runner hit a rock outcrop head-on, and flipped end for end, landing on the roof. Thanks to airbags, a seat belt and a tremendous amount of good luck, I crawled out the passenger side window of the smashed vehicle unharmed. But the lesson was stamped into my brain like a rumble strip in the asphalt: slow down. Seat belts are mandatory, of course, but paying attention to the weather and road conditions can mean the difference between bringing your kid home for Christmas and a tragedy that will shatter your family.

I've passed that curve in I-90 many times since that crash, and I always get a chill. But my carelessness didn't change the striking beauty of that drive. You can feel the gain in elevation as you climb toward Lookout Pass at the north end of the Bitterroot Mountains as the band of big sky narrows, visible through a shrinking space between the encroaching trees. The smell of the woods is bracing here—pine, larch, aspens, cottonwoods, and usually a trace of smoke, whether from summer wildfires or cozy wood stoves burning in the winter. When the sun is low on the horizon the shadows grow long and the trees stand in sharp relief, and it's easy to imagine that the forest goes on forever.

These are just a few pink lines in a state full of amazing stretches of roadway that can make your journey every bit as entertaining and memorable as your destination. You can be in a hurry somewhere else. Give Montana a chance to sink in.

The Bitterroot Mountains, in the distance, frame the Bitterroot River, one of the more popular summer destinations in Glacier Country.

GLACIER COUNTRY

GLACIER NATIONAL PARK TAKES UP LESS than ten percent of the slice of northwest Montana called Glacier Country, which might suggest the tourism handle is a misnomer for the rest of the region. A peek at some historical geology, though, shows it to be an apt descriptor for all of Montana's mountainous northwest.

In Missoula, you can easily see the evidence of a glacial lake in the horizontal strandlines etched into the slope of Mount Sentinel. Glacial Lake Missoula existed at the end of the Pleistocene era, a series of ice ages that ended about 11,000 years ago, and eventually receded to allow room for espresso shops, pop-up art galleries, medical marijuana dispensaries, and RV dealerships. Skiers and snowboarders don't have far to drive with Snowbowl ski area on the south end of the valley. Missoula is also the cultural hub of the Northern Rockies, bursting with art shows, live theatre, big-name concerts, and a number of unique events that reflect the strong hippie ethos that still shapes much of this vibrant University town.

A more traditional version of Montana exists in the heavily forested northwest area of Glacier Country, west of the national park. Libby and Eureka have always been blue collar industry towns, built around vermiculite mining and logging, respectively. The mining didn't end well, with asbestos in the vermiculite creating massive health problems for miners and residents, contributing to hundreds of deaths. The mine is now a Superfund site. Environmental concerns have also severely reduced logging in the region, with both towns still reeling from the severe decline in that industry. Times are changing, though, in Glacier Country. Perhaps more than anywhere else in Montana, tourism has replaced the extractive industries at the top of the economic food chain here. Flathead Lake, like Glacier and Yellowstone National Parks, has rarely had a problem drawing a crowd. The largest natural body of fresh water west of the Mississippi, it's a remnant of Glacial Lake Missoula. Somers, Lakeside, and Big Arm along the west shore are hopping in the summer with visitors who sail, waterski, fish for lake trout, or just putter around on pontoon boats taking in the splendor of the Mission Mountains to the east. Polson, on the lake's southern end, bustles year-round, as does Big Fork on the northeast shore. Montanans have a keen affection for Flathead Lake, and efforts are continuing to try and eradicate the non-native lake trout and to keep disastrous aquatic invasive species like zebra mussels from being introduced.

Outdoors enthusiasts will find some of the best hiking and camping in the Bitterroot Mountains that snake along the border between Montana and Idaho. The Bitterroot Valley is an important agricultural piece of the rural picture and the gorgeous valley makes for one of the most soul-nourishing drives in the state, any time of year along State Highway 93 South.

Like the park it's named for, Glacier Country offers a diversity of experiences and landscapes, with some of the most dramatic scenery in the West. And the people here, from a curator at the Museum of the Plains Indian in Browning to a brewery taproom manager in Darby, are as genuine and laid back as you'll find.

A MOREL IMPERATIVE

IN WESTERN MONTANA, THE 2017 FIRE SEASON was one of the worst in more than one hundred years. Persistent drought conditions provided plenty of fuel for wildfires, which were started by lightning and such human causes as carelessly tossed cigarettes and untended campfires. By the time a series of weather systems brought enough rain and snow to snuff out most of the fires in late September, nearly 1.3 million acres of Montana had burned, the most since the Great Burn of 1910, which torched more than 3 million acres across Western Montana, North Idaho, and Eastern Washington. In 2017 hundreds of people, including the entire town of Seeley Lake, were evacuated from their homes. Dozens of outbuildings and houses were destroyed. Two wildland firefighters lost their lives that summer, and state officials reported that the total cost of fire suppression was almost $400 million.

It was a grim summer, to be sure. Residents of the Northern Rockies, especially those who live along the wildland interface, know that each summer brings a potential for devastating wildfires. Fire is, of course, an integral part of the natural cycle of regeneration for forests, and the debate over logging and suppression rages on. There's one byproduct of Montana's wildfires, however, that is hotly anticipated each year by a legion of intrepid hunters: mushrooms. The brown morel, to be specific. Thousands of "morelers" will flood into Lolo, Kootenai, and other National Forests of Glacier Country each spring, scouring the burned timber areas for the tasty delicacy.

The fungal object that engenders this fanaticism looks like an elongated doorknob that's made of lasagna noodles. Their vague resemblance to a pine cone is the perfect camouflage in the coniferous forests they prefer. Their incredible flavor makes them the most sought-after of the edible wild mushrooms, bringing as much as $8 per pound of fresh picked morels, up to $150 per pound dried. With that much potential cash lying around the forests, competition for their harvest is fierce. 'Shroom hunters are as tight-lipped about their productive spots as fishermen are with a favorite meat hole. Armed with enough knowledge and planning, though, even first-timers can have a pretty good chance of bringing home some morels on their first excursion.

"It's like a treasure hunt," says Deserae King, an avid mushroom hunter who learned at the feet of Larry Evans, the celebrated mycologist from Missoula. "Everybody knows where the burns are. You just have to hike farther than the other hunters. I've put in sixteen to twenty miles a day hunting mushrooms." King, a Missoula photographer, has developed a sixth sense for locating her quarry. "My nickname is Truffles," she laughs. "I have a very keen sense of smell."

It's not just morels that bring her back to the woods every spring, she adds. Experienced 'shroomers also collect oyster mushrooms, boletes, puffballs, lobster mushrooms, and her favorite, chanterelles. One of the larger edibles is known as the chicken of the woods. They are typically found on the side of a tree, growing outward in wavy fans of flesh, yellow-beige in color and shaped like a large, leafy head of lettuce. "They're treated as meat by vegans," King says. "I like to cut them into strips and sauté them. It has the texture and quality of chicken."

Larry Evans is a quirky character who frequently writes songs about his favorite fungi when he's not teaching workshops and leading forest forays all over the world. His evangelical fervor is plain in the lyrics of his songs, which are packed with information like where to search for certain species, as in "Chanterelle:"

I like old growth habitat, and that is where I am at/
Where the trees are big and fat.

But, as Evans is quick to caution, you can't just go out there and start popping every mushroom into your mouth. "You can eat any mushroom," he says. "Once." Enthusiasts must be knowledgeable in mushroom identification, as many species can be deadly poisonous. Even the morel, if eaten uncooked, can cause gastric distress. True morels

The "chicken of the wood" mushroom, which tastes like meat when properly prepared, is highly prized for its flavor. Photo © Deserae King

have a spongy, honeycombed cap with a stem attached directly to the bottom. False morels have a more muddled texture and can be poisonous. One sure way to tell them apart is to slice them in half. True morels are hollow. Another reliable trick for identifying poisonous mushrooms is to check underneath the cap. Most edible mushrooms have a spongy, porous texture, whereas poisonous mushrooms tend to have gills, a radial pattern of thin flukes. There are exceptions, a few edible species that also have gills, but for those who are not experienced mycologists, it's an easy rule of thumb, although not a substitute for boning up on the positive identification of mushroom species.

In 2017 some 700,000 acres of Forest Service Region One had burned to provide the perfect hunting ground for morels. That's a lot of real estate to comb for morels and other edible forest fungi. So how does a 'shroomer narrow it down and increase their chances of scoring some specimens? Other than a burn site, one good bet is sticking to river bottoms that have a lot of cottonwood. It's a favored environment for morels. Usually it's the naturals, or golden-colored morels that tend to pop here after the first warm spring day. Evans says he also looks for *Mycelium,* little white filaments growing on the underside of logs that signal the probable presence of morels. And when one morel is found, it pays to search a twenty-foot radius around it. They tend to grow in clusters.

The Forest Service issues permits for gathering mushrooms, as the fungi are considered a forest product. No permit is needed for incidental use, which is up to five gallons gathered over the course of a season. Permits are required but issued at no charge for up to 20 gallons per season for personal use. A $20 permit will allow an individual to gather up to 20 gallons for resale, and there is a limit of $300 of these permits per season. Commercial permits are also available, and information on those fees can be found at the Northern Region's mushroom site online.

IN BROWNING, IF YOU CAN'T BEAT 'EM, BUY 'EM

IMAGINE TURNING ON YOUR KITCHEN FAUCET and nothing comes out. Dry as a bone. How are you supposed to make coffee? Do laundry? Make dinner for your family? Imagine it isn't the first time it's happened. Your town's water supply has become pretty dicey, but also expensive. The situation is untenable—your family needs reliable water service. So, what do you do?

You could buy the town.

At least that's what the Blackfeet Nation had in mind when they decided to purchase the assets of the town of Browning in 2017. The hub of activity on the res, Browning, about 48 miles south of the Canadian border just east of Glacier National Park, is home to about one thousand people. It's also a town that's deeply troubled. Unemployment hovers between 65 and 70 percent, and the average annual income is somewhere around $13,000, well below Montana's poverty line for a two-person household. As with most reservation towns, the conditions are abysmal. Alcoholism and drug abuse are off the charts. Tribe-owned housing units are decrepit, poorly insulated, and frequently overcrowded. Inadequate federal funding can't keep pace with the need for repairs to existing houses, let alone pay for the construction of new ones. It's a dire situation that traps many tribal members who can't find a way off the res, and it's been that way for decades.

The Blackfeet, with a tribal membership of about 10,000 on a reservation slightly larger than Glacier National Park, with which it shares a border, saw an opportunity to at least seize control of the utilities situation when the city of Browning found itself in debt to the tribe's Two Medicine Water Company (TMWC) to the tune of $1.8 million. The town also owed debts to other tribal entities totaling about $825,000. In August of 2017 the Blackfeet, through their economic development arm, the Si-yeh Corporation, agreed to assume these debts, and in exchange would receive the "right, title and interest" to the town's assets, valued at $9,714,885. Had the tribe not stepped in, most of that debt would have likely reverted to Glacier County. As the consequences of the deal continue to unfold, though, it may have turned out to be a short-sighted move that could leave the tribe in even worse shape than before.

The water supply was just one of the issues that the tribe now had to address, and it would prove to be a complex problem with no easy solution. "The city of Browning was forever having problems with their water system," says Chips Running Crane, a Blackfeet tribal member who works for Indian Health Services in Browning. "It was bad. The wells would run dry, and people would be out of water for a while. They would have to drill another well and hopefully would hit something, and they would pull in that water." The $22 million Blackfeet Community Water System was completed in 2012, but the city—which had provided water to the residents since 1934—couldn't afford to maintain it and began falling behind in their payments to the TMWC. In an attempt to recoup payments from the water users, the Blackfeet Tribal Business Council allegedly began using a customer list obtained from the city to get the addresses of the city's water customers. In a lawsuit filed by the city of Browning in 2014, they allege that the Council began sending notices to these customers requesting them to send utility payments directly to TMWC, bypassing the city.

The Tribal Business Council is just one entity of many who have a dog in this fight, but there is no clearcut hegemony with the multiple jurisdictional layers involved in Indian reservation business. The sovereign nation is a federally recognized entity, much like a military base. But overlaid on that jurisdiction are the rules of the state of Montana, Glacier County, and the city of Browning. The entanglements and contradictions among the different factions involved are extremely difficult to navigate, and no one seems to have all the answers to any question that comes up. Before the sale, Browning's city council, for example, had no tribal members. Conversely, in Cut Bank, the county seat, the county commission is mostly made up of Blackfeet Indians. Federal employees like Chips cannot officially participate in tribal politics, even when they are tribal members. "It is really hard," he says. "The reservation and the county have a very extensive dysfunctional relationship. We run against everything that the state does, being considered essentially a semi-autonomous country."

One of the reasons the tribe cut the deal with the city in the first place was to head off the city's proposed flat rate of $150 a month per household for water service, a rate most of the impoverished residents could not afford. Current rates are around fifty dollars. Browning is one of Montana's poorest towns, and their economy relies largely on business from the seasonal traffic passing through on the way to or from Glacier National Park. The embattled city, full of struggling, white-owned businesses, simply

Blackfeet artist Jay Laber has used junk vehicles found on the reservation to create the warriors that stand guard at each entrance to the Blackfeet Nation, east of Glacier Park.

couldn't maintain or expand the new system without increasing the rates. The immediate goal of water security was the carrot that brought the tribe to the bargaining table to explore the option of buying the town and its assets, but thus far the aftermath of the deal, including the dissolution of Browning's city government in February of 2018, has produced far more problems than it has solved.

When Siyeh announced the new lease of up to $1200 a month for an office space that, before the city dissolved, had been leased to the county for one dollar per year, the county yanked its services in Browning. The satellite county offices closed down. Now residents would have to drive to Cut Bank, a 70-mile round trip, for things like driver's licenses and vehicle registration. Volunteer firefighters have reportedly been filling the fuel tanks of fire trucks—which the tribe now owns—out of their own pockets. As the tribe struggles with issues like finding offices for the monthly county commission meetings, which have been hosted in restaurants and even private homes, the situation is a hot button mess with no clear path forward.

This appears to be the only instance in U.S. history where a tribal nation has purchased a town from a government entity. Although the situation is unique to the Blackfeet Nation, one of Montana's seven reservations, they share the bigger issues faced by all tribes as they struggle for survival and recognition. Browning's drinking water issue is just one of hundreds of crushing problems facing Native Americans not just in Montana, but across the U.S., as Native Americans try to survive in a culture that has surrounded them with obstacles but offers little in the way of help or understanding. The Blackfeet people continue to fight for basic access to clean drinking water, something most of us take for granted. Chips Running Crane remains hopeful, though, citing the promise of fresh perspectives from the three new council members who were sworn in to the Tribal Council during Browning's 2018 Indian Days. "We're constantly changing. There's never been a time when the tribe has been just stagnant. It is going to change. I think the tribe is starting to realize that they've taken on something that is almost too big to swallow. But they can't deny it now. They can't just look away and say, we can't deal with it. They have to deal with it."

A delicately lettered warning to local law enforcement adorns a home on the Blackfeet Reservation in Browning.

HOT SPRINGS AND COOL ART

THE TOWN OF HOT SPRINGS IS A GREAT PLACE to get away, whether for a few days or a few decades. Just inside the western edge of the Flathead Reservation, the charming town of 600 denizens has long been recognized as not just a place to soak in the steaming mineral pools, but as a hotbed of the quirky and creative, a vibrant community of artists and colorful characters who share an affinity for the isolation and singular, funky vibe.

Don't bother with your cell phone here. Service is sketchy, even with the recently installed cell tower that was fought against tooth and nail by a contingent of locals who prefer to keep the larger grid at arm's length. Besides, the communications network here is robust and reliable. When a hot nugget of gossip pops up in the organic grocery or a Main Street watering hole, its value is immediately assessed. Did it come from a local? From well-regarded regular from out of town? Or is it just some empty conjecture uttered by a rubbernecker passing through? If it's deemed reliable intel it's elevated from random scuttlebutt into the grapevine, where status updates can travel faster than an Instagram post. Hot Springs is a closed system, and in a small town like this, everybody knows everybody else's business. It can be nigh impossible to achieve much anonymity, but for the most part they seem to enjoy the familiarity. There are no secrets, and that somehow adds to the mystique. It is like a groovy oasis, this little Montana town where residents dig life on "Hot Springs time," and visitors come to immerse themselves in its eccentric charm.

Hot Springs lies several miles off the beaten path but has thrived through more than a century of good times and bad. Situated snugly in the Little Bitterroot Valley just east of Baldy Mountain off State Highway 28, the town started out as Pineville in the 1890s, right next to another little town called Camas Hot Springs. Pineville—by then called Hot Springs—incorporated in 1929. Business-gutting fires, sawmill closures, and other hardships had the population as low as 400 in 1990, but a scrappy core of determined souls have kept Hot Springs chugging along. Civic pride is alive and well, on display at the annual rodeo and Homesteader Days. Some locals, like Rick DePoe, Hot Springs High School class of 1976, never saw a reason to leave. "It's an easy town to live in. I love it."

*Hot Springs artist Joan
Nevarez talks about one of her
paintings at her farm complex
near Lonepine Reservoir.*

The stubborn spirit of the pioneers lives on perhaps most strongly in the artistic community that's thrived here for as long as anyone can remember. Nick Barber and Abby Coleman, owners of the Barber Shop Beer Parlor, succumbed to the pull of Hot Springs's oddball charm after living in various parts of the Flathead Valley, although, Nick says, Hot Springs takes some attitude adjustment. "You've got to find the right mindset to live here day to day." Abby likes the tight-knit community, where she feels comfortable letting her two grade-school kids ramble around town unchaperoned. Neighbors keep her apprised of their whereabouts, and she does the same with their kids. The lifestyle suits her. "I couldn't do the nine-to-five," she says.

Scattered among the hills around town and tucked away among the pines in back-yards are dozens of artists' studios, where Hot Springs artists surrender to their muse. Their work is well-represented in businesses around town, as well as in public spaces like the library and post office. The Hot Springs Artists Society is instrumental in keeping the arts scene going, sponsoring weekly live music performances and other cultural events where local art can be purchased.

Nothing represents the iconoclastic tribe of Hot Springs' artists better than the renegade who blazes her own trail. Joan Nevarez is just such an artist, and for 18 years she's been a colorful Hot Springs fixture. The 72-year-old painter lives in a bright pink farm house about eight miles out of town, sharing her spread with pigs, llamas, peacocks, chickens, geese, a rambunctious black dog named Puppy, a donkey or two, and goats. Lots of goats.

Her property sits in the shadow of an earthen dam that forms Lonepine Reservoir. She welcomed this visitor on a recent fall day, just after she'd returned from picking apples. A dozen escaped goats march single file along the road atop the dam while another herd of bleating fugitives works their way in the opposite direction, munching knapweed on the slope below them. Lying in the shade of a fruit tree near the irrigation ditch just below the dam, Puppy gnaws contentedly on the horn of a goat skull.

"Are you interested in goats?" Nevarez says by way of greeting. Her silver hair banded into loose ponytails, she wears two sweaters against the early-autumn chill. Several colorful tchotchkes hang on leather thongs around her neck, her glasses secured to a braided cord with duct tape. Her guarded smile and laughing hazel eyes signal a playful spirit. In Hot Springs she's known as the Goat Lady, a nickname she dismisses with a wave. "Some young child gave me that name." It doesn't take much coaxing before she nips back into the farmhouse and emerges with some clay sculptures and paintings to show off. She grew up with an aunt in West Virginia, she says, who made porcelain dolls. It made an impression on the young free spirit who eventually found her way to Hot Springs by way of Bozeman. While she goes through "phases" of working with clay, painting is her main passion.

"When I paint, I can forget about all my worries and problems. I guess it's a form of meditation," she says. In order to get some work done before her menagerie starts crying for food, she arises before 5:00 a.m. each day and paints until the sun comes up. "I don't know what I'd do if I couldn't paint," she says. "It's just part of my blood."

Like many Hot Springs artists, Nevarez paints for the love of art, but wouldn't mind selling some more of her work too. Her subject matter frequently depicts scenes from the town itself, and several of her paintings hang in businesses on Main Street in a sort of meta display. She also sells prints, the most popular of which is a depiction of the stalwart Montana Bar. She traded the original painting for a bale of hay. "Money is a funny commodity out here," she says, regarding sluggish sales.

With its small, nearly static population and its location away from the tourist-heavy routes that lead to Glacier or Yellowstone, Hot Springs can be a tough town in which to make a living as an artist. That doesn't seem to slow down the army of creators who craft jewelry, pottery, paintings, sculptures, murals and rustic pieces assembled from found objects. "There's lots of talent here," says Nevarez. For most of them, an austere lifestyle is a fair trade for being able to live in a unique community that's relaxed and close-knit, where people can do what they want, and neighbors have each other's backs. Most of the Hot Springs folks you talk to are friendly and welcoming, and they seem to have that artist's knack of recognizing the beauty in nearly everything around them. That works just fine for Joan Nevarez. "I like artists. If the world had more artists in it, it would be a better world."

THE RISE AND FALL OF MILLTOWN DAM

FOR MOST OF THE TWENTIETH CENTURY, Missoula rolled along, gradually moving away from its industrial roots as a railroad and timber town towards its current incarnation as Montana's hipster hub of arts and culture—all the while sitting just seven miles downstream from a ticking time bomb. A few people knew it was there, but it wasn't until 1996 that the broader public became aware of the potential disaster trapped at the confluence of two rivers.

Let's backtrack a bit. For as long as 10,000 years, the confluence of the Blackfoot River and the Clark Fork has been a popular site, a good fishing hole for native peoples to stop and harvest fish on their way to the buffalo hunting plains of the east. The Salish word for the area, *Naaycčstm*, means "place of the mature bull trout." Once the discovery of gold in the mid-1800s started bringing miners into the area, the rivers were seen as a different kind of resource, a mechanical one.

Butte, 120 miles upstream, became the biggest mining operation in America in the late-nineteenth and early twentieth-centuries, producing the copper needed for wiring America with electricity. Mining also produced millions of tons of arsenic, manganese, lead, and cadmium—dangerous heavy metals and toxins in the mining tailings which were discharged from the Butte operations into Silver Bow Creek, which dumped into the Clark Fork near the smelter town of Anaconda.

A channel of the Blackfoot River, in the upper right, flows freely into the Clark Fork for the first time in 100 years. Photo © Jonathan Qualben

In 1908 the Milltown Dam was constructed at the confluence, with the goal of providing hydroelectricity to Butte mining magnate William A. Clark's Missoula-Bonner trolley line and possibly to Bonner and Milltown, where timbers were milled and shipped to Butte for mine construction. Within six months of the dam's completion, however, the old Yiddish saying, "man plans, God laughs," was exemplified when massive spring flooding washed more than six million tons of toxic mining waste miles down the Clark Fork from Butte, where it settled in the reservoir behind Milltown Dam.

For decades, the official line on the 540-acre reservoir was to let sleeping dogs lie. Then, in 1981 Missoula County drew routine water samples from seven drinking water wells in Milltown, and four of the wells—serving 35 households—were found to be contaminated with ten times the EPA-allowed limit of arsenic. The poisonous gunk lurking in Milltown Reservoir was leaching into the groundwater. In 1983 the state filed a lawsuit against ARCO, which had bought the Anaconda Minerals Company, and the Milltown Dam complex was placed on the EPA's National Priorities List. A feasibility study was funded to determine the best course of action for remediation; the EPA capped the wells and looked for a new drinking water supply for Bonner and Milltown.

Once again, the rivers refused to recognize manmade timelines. In February of 1996 thick ice on the Blackfoot broke up and a ten-mile ice jam flowed downstream scouring the river bottoms, wiping out the fisheries and threatening to push the Milltown Dam to its capacity and beyond. Before ice and water could fill the reservoir, workers opened the floodgates and allowed water from the reservoir to wash downstream through Missoula, toxic sludge and all. The poisoned water choked the river, killing thousands of fish. It was a shocking wake-up call. Nearly seven million tons of toxic waste still sat behind the aging dam, poised to bring an environmental catastrophe to Montana's third largest city. Missoula's pristine aquifer, which provided clean drinking water to 100,000 people, hung in the balance. If the Milltown Dam gave way, it would be one of the worst environmental disasters since, well, Butte.

At that point the saga of Milltown Dam became a tug-of-war between the state, the EPA, the Clark Fork Coalition, Montana's governor, a powerful Montana industrialist, and the residents of several communities along the Clark Fork who would be directly impacted by whatever plan was put in motion to clean up the Milltown Reservoir.

The line of the former Milltown Dam can be traced to the far bank of the Clark Fork, in this view from the Milltown State Park.

Gary Matson lives in Bonner, and in 2001 he helped form the science-based Bonner Development Group, a small coalition whose purpose was to identify the facts of the situation at a time when the key players were putting out a lot of misinformation. Matson's group had yet to be convinced that dredging the reservoir—which was recommended by environmentalists and political leaders—was the proper tack, and were determined to keep the dam. The BDG sided with ARCO, which had inherited the pond and its toxic sediment when it bought Anaconda Copper Company in 1977, and wanted to leave the sediment in place, so as not to stir up the toxins into the pond and send them downstream. "People kayaked on that reservoir," said Matson. "There were cranes, all kinds of birds. Because it was a 'run of the river' dam (a hydroelectric dam with little or no water storage), there were small levels of toxicity (in the surface water) but not enough to be dangerous."

Another group of Bonner neighbors had been meeting in living rooms to hash out the possible solutions, and in 2002 Friends of Two Rivers was born. They took a different view from the BDG, advocating for the removal of the dam and the restoration of the confluence to its natural state. Governor Judy Martz threw her weight behind the cleanup scenario, and the EPA soon followed suit with a proposal for the dam removal and cleanup of the area. By this time the reservoir had been declared a federal Superfund site, part of the Clark Fork Complex stretching 140 miles up to Butte. It was the largest Superfund complex in the nation and ARCO was officially on the hook for removing all the toxic material from the pond.

Work began on removing the sediment from behind the dam, and Missoula's Clark Fork Coalition, among others, was instrumental in getting the state on board. Even Gary Matson eventually came around to the anti-dam way of thinking, and joined forces with Friends of Two Rivers, and they wanted the Milltown Dam gone. Their reasoning was sound: Every few years produced enough rain and subsequent snowmelt to repeat the floods or ice jams that could threaten the structure. After a huge amount of arm-twisting and political maneuvering, much of it coming from the Clark Fork Coalition, the state agreed that the Milltown Dam would be removed, and proposed a river restoration plan that included returning a natural-flowing channel to the Clark Fork. In March of 2008, after one hundred years of the dam's existence and more than ten years of struggle over getting it removed, a small coffer dam was breached, and the Blackfoot flowed through a channel into the Clark Fork. The old powerhouse, a much-loved local landmark, was demolished. The rest of the dam was eventually dismantled and entirely removed. The sediment that had been laboriously dredged from behind the dam had been sent back upstream in railcars owned by Missoula industrialist Denny Washington, who also owned Envirocon, which had received the contract for the cleanup. In a stunning stroke of what can be seen either as irony, cruelty, or twisted poetic logic, the more than two million cubic yards of toxic waste removed from the reservoir were shipped a hundred miles upstream to Opportunity and spread into tailing ponds that already existed there, originally built to take smelting waste from Anaconda. The area near Opportunity was already polluted beyond repair, it was decided, so the waste would just add to the existing pile. The 300 residents of Opportunity objected but were overruled. Montana's Department of Environmental Quality oversaw the project.

Reclamation efforts involved the engineering and design of a new river channel for the Clark Fork upstream from the reservoir as part of the transformation of the reservoir back into its original state as a floodplain. Bends were designed into the channel, and large boulders were placed to guide the water's flow.

Tree stumps that poked out of the reservoir bottom a hundred years ago can be seen now on the floodplain south of I-90. The area is covered with willows and other vegetation, and in time those black stumps will be replaced naturally by their living counterparts.

The final phase of the Milltown Project is redevelopment, which includes a state park. Jean Curtiss, a Missoula County Commissioner who left office in 2018 after serving three terms, is pleased with the results. "One of my biggest concerns was getting the confluence developed into a park. As the I-90 bridges are replaced, a trail from the new state park will go under the Interstate bridges and the railroad bridge to Highway 200 and the little park. So my concerns have been addressed over time." Although some ideas, such as a kayak play wave, were ditched along the way, Curtiss is happy with the outcome. "Originally it was thought to be more of a local park but becoming a state park is great," she says. Milltown State Park is now Montana's second largest state park, behind Makoshika State Park in eastern Montana. Blacktop paths wind past picnic shelters around the confluence area, dotted with interpretive signs that explain the history. "It's a tremendously powerful message," says Matson of the restored confluence. "It's kind of a rebirth of a floodplain and a naturally running river."

Across the Clark Fork, up on a bluff, an overlook affords the clearest view of the Blackfoot flowing underneath the I-90 bridge and quietly joining Montana's biggest river which continues to do what a river does, carrying water from the mountains to the sea.

MONTANA'S MOST UNWELCOME VISITOR?

IF YOU'RE PLANNING A VISIT TO MONTANA, there's something you're absolutely forbidden to bring with you. It's tiny, no bigger than two inches, and if you do bring it, chances are you won't even know you're carrying it. Believe it or not, though, it has the power of causing billions of dollars' worth of damage.

Got your attention? If you are a Montanan, you probably already know I'm talking about the zebra mussel. This little bivalve, *Dreissena polymorpha*, (and its smaller relative the quaggy mussel) is an invasive aquatic species (AIS) that has already wreaked havoc in the Great Lakes, Midwest watersheds, and the Colorado River Basin, and threatens to make its way into Big Sky Country. The little striped buggers reproduce extremely quickly and usually are found in clusters of up to 10,000 mussels per square foot, massed around hard surfaces like hydroelectric stations and other underwater structures, creating major headaches. They're typically moved from one body of water

The Flathead Lake Biological Station, on Yellow Bay south of Bigfork, is on the front lines in the battle against the zebra mussel, an invasive species.
Photo © Troy Schlimgen

to another by attaching themselves to boat hulls, trailers and motors or inside bilge pumps. Once out of the water, they can stay alive for weeks. Millions of dollars have already been spent in states where AIS infestations have clogged municipal pipes, hydraulic facilities and agricultural machinery. Thus far in Montana, we've been lucky—not a single adult mussel has been found in our waters.

There have already been many non-native species introduced to Montana waters by sloppy sportsmen or so-called bucket biologists. Some bodies of water like Flathead Lake currently have more non-native fish, like lake trout, dominating the biological community. Northern pike have also been artificially introduced and now occur in most Montana watersheds, where their predation on other species has put a significant dent in the trout fishery on many prime trout streams. But it's not sheer luck that's kept the zebra mussels out of western Montana's watershed. It's taken a lot of hard work, coordination, funding, and persistence from several entities on the front lines of this potentially devastating invader.

Nestled among the pines on the north shore of Flathead Lake's Yellow Bay is the Flathead Lake Biological Station, and aside from the maroon oval sign at the entrance on Highway 35, you'd never know it was there. Low slung taupe buildings with green metal roofs contain laboratories, classrooms, and administrative offices. A series of cabins for visiting students and researchers is stashed among the trees along the point that encloses Yellow Bay. According to one Bio Station employee, people who live on Yellow Bay don't even know they're there, and yet the Station has become the sentinel of the lake's water quality. What started as a tent on the Swan River in 1899 has grown into a state-of-the-art facility that has forged a worldwide network of scientists and water quality experts, with a focus on the health of the Flathead watershed. Part of the University of Montana, the facility has worked to stay a step ahead of perceived environmental threats to the lake.

Now the Bio Station has brought the weight of its expertise and resources to bear on the zebra mussel threat. According to Tom Bansak, Assistant Director of the Bio Station, in the fall of 2016 juvenile dreissenid mussels were detected by Montana Fish, Wildlife & Parks in the Tiber Reservoir near Chester and in Canyon Ferry Reservoir near Helena. "In the battle against these mussels, early detection is the name of the game" says Bansak. "Since people are the vector of spread, we must also be the solution." To that end, the Bio Station has teamed up with other groups who are invested in the health of the lake and its watershed. The Confederated Salish Kootenai

Tribes and Whitefish Lake Institute have joined the effort, and the state Department of Natural Resources and Conservation is providing funding for such things as the statewide watercraft inspection campaign.

On a Thursday afternoon in July, a maroon SUV with Kalispell plates pulls into a watercraft inspection station between Browning and East Glacier. Shawna, one of the inspectors, brushes a bit of dirt off her neon-green vest as she asks the driver where the boat is coming from, and he tells her McGregor Lake. Going to the Missouri, he says. Her partner Wendy inspects the hull of the boat, the lower part of the outboard motor, and then opens the lid on the live well and finds it empty. Shawna stamps the driver's inspection passport and send him on his way. He probably doesn't know there's another inspection coming up on the other side of Browning.

"The first year we only had an inspection station at the buffalo pasture (west of Browning)," says site supervisor Jay Monroe. "Now there's two in Browning, a mandatory station westbound at East Seville, Highway 89 in Birch Creek—we do about 187 inspections in a day." The discoveries of mussels at Tiber and Canyon Ferry, he adds, triggered five years of study there and impelled the state to free up funding to expand the inspection program. Thanks to a partnership with Fish, Wildlife and Parks, there are more than 30 inspection stations throughout the state, including stations along each border. All watercraft, including canoes, kayaks and paddleboards, are required to stop for inspection.

"The good news is that most Montanans are aware of the issues with mussels. But not all," says Norma Nickerson, director of UM's Institute for Tourism Recreation Research. She's hoping the Institute's efforts to raise public awareness of the danger of invasive mussels through billboards and increased news coverage will continue to get the word out. The "Clean. Drain. Dry." campaign seems to be getting some traction. "My belief is it's a very good success story," she says.

During the 2018 season, over fifty thousand boats were inspected. Twelve were found to be carrying invasive mussels into the state. These infested boats were treated with superheated water and locked to their trailers for a 30-day quarantine.

If only one boat gets through and deposits zebra mussels into Montana waters, it could set off a catastrophic chain of events. A single female *Dreissena* can produce a million young over its four-to-five-year lifespan, and once a population is established it is an ecological nightmare. Mussels feed on huge amounts of plankton, robbing many established species of their food source. They have no predators. And

once they're established, removing them is like putting toothpaste back in the tube. A nascent population will have to be detected and eradicated immediately; no zebra mussel colony has successfully been removed from an area bigger than 30 acres.

Western states in the Columbia River watershed, which is fed by Montana's rivers, are also watching our situation closely. If the zebra mussel infestation spreads to the Columbia River Basin, it could cost that region's power producers $90 million a year to keep their facilities functioning properly. Those added costs would be passed directly to the consumer, which would potentially wind up costing the Pacific Northwest five to six billion dollars.

That's a lot of damage wrought by an animal the size of your thumb.

GRIZZLIES: COMING TO A FIELD NEAR YOU?

In a glass display case at the Basin Trading Post in Stanford, a six-foot-long white wolf holds a predatory pose. Head down, ears back, its black lips are pulled back over a big mouthful of sharp teeth. For at least fifteen years in the early twentieth century, the rare white wolf nicknamed the White Ghost terrorized ranchers between the Highwood and Little Belt Mountains in central Montana, killing more than $30,000 worth of sheep and calves while eluding traps, poisoned bait, hunters, dogs, even aerial pursuit before finally being shot by Al Close in 1930. The White Ghost is Stanford's claim to fame, the most formidable predator to ever roam the Judith Gap.

Until now. Shock waves rippled through Montana's ranching community when two grizzly bears were euthanized in June of 2017 after killing four calves just west of Stanford. It was the first time grizzlies had been seen this far east in more than a century. The sub-adult males had come from the Northern Continental Divide Ecosystem (NCDE) which extends along the Northern Front of the Rockies from

Montana has more grizzly bears than any state in the Lower 48, but their continued recovery and management are the source of great controversy.
Photo courtesy of 123rf.com © byrdyak

Glacier Park down to the southern tip of the Bob Marshall Wilderness Complex. A year later, a grizzly killed a calf on a ranch just north of Two Dot, about fifty miles south of Stanford. These incidents, along with several reported sightings in other areas east of the Northern Front, make it clear that the grizzlies have not only bounced back from being placed on the Endangered Species list in 1975, but they're actually expanding their territory. Montana's biggest apex predator has state and federal wildlife agencies asking the question, how many grizzlies are enough grizzlies?

A better question to ask might be: Why are they expanding their territory? The short answer, according to Keith Hammer of the Swan View Coalition, is food. "Grizzlies are expanding their range due to changes in climate and available foods, not simply due to expanding numbers as government agencies would have us believe," he says. "The greatest expansion in range in Yellowstone, for example, has occurred during a period where the population level remained flat." Warmer temperatures and shorter winters are causing smaller crops of berries and other vegetation, forcing the bears to move into new territory in search of food. Climate change also affects the migratory patterns of bison, one of the grizzly's biggest sources of protein, and as they thin out in their normal territory, the bears take more livestock.

Before hunters caused a steep decline in their numbers in the early twentieth century, more than fifty thousand grizzly bears—a subspecies of brown bear—inhabited the Greater Yellowstone Ecosystem (GYE), which, at 34,375 square miles, is one of the largest temperate-zone ecosystems on earth. By 1975 that number had plummeted to 136 individuals, which landed the bears on the "threatened" list under the Endangered Species Act. Today there are about 700 grizzlies in the GYE, a rebound that has been credited to the recovery efforts and protection afforded by their ESA designation. The U.S. Fish and Wildlife Service (USFWS) considered this such a conservation success story, in fact, that they removed the GYE grizzly population from the "threatened" list in 2007. Conservations groups filed lawsuits immediately, and the fate of the grizzlies has been threading its way through the courts ever since.

While the GYE doesn't have the largest population of bears—the NCDE contains about one thousand grizzlies—it does involve three states, Idaho, Montana and Wyoming. In 2017 Department of the Interior Secretary Ryan

Zinke announced that the USFWS would once again be delisting the Greater Yellowstone grizzlies, and a management plan in the form of special grizzly bear hunts in Wyoming and Idaho was put into play. Environmental groups, teaming up with a number of Native American tribes, again filed suit. Bonnie Rice of the Sierra Club's grizzly bear program said the delisting would undo the progress that had been made over the previous forty years. "This decision is extremely premature and could set grizzly bear recovery in the Yellowstone region back by decades." Tim Preso, an attorney for EarthJustice saw the delisting as a response to arm-twisting from the state agencies. "Fish and Wildlife have been moving this direction under pressure from the states." Continued protection for the GYE population, he said, would allow the long-term natural migration to develop. "Now there's an opportunity to link up the Yellowstone population to the northern population and open the door for bears to recolonize central Idaho, more of their historical habitat." From a biological standpoint, if the grizzlies continue to wander farther outside their original territory, the lines of the distinct populations may eventually begin to blur. But they won't be able to make those long, multi-season journeys between ecosystems without the ESA providing continued protection that will allow the bears to inhabit the areas in between the NCDE and the GYE. "Without ESA protection," says Hammer, "these bears will be relocated or shot."

Nearly drowned out in much of the back-and-forth between government agencies and environmental groups has been the voice of Montana's Native American tribes. North America's indigenous peoples have never seen the grizzly bear as a resource to be managed any more than we need to manage the stars or the wind. Johnny Arlee, a spiritual leader and tribal elder with the Confederated Salish and Kootenai tribes from the Flathead Indian reservation, made plain his disgust with those who would treat the creature as a commodity. "My message to trophy hunters who want to kill this sacred being on our sacred lands is this: Go home," he said in 2016. "It's crazy to have these rich white people coming here to kill, kill, kill and to brag about killing a grizzly bear. Human beings are crazy. There has got to be a change in our heart. If it was turned around the other way and the trophy hunters were hunted, it would be a different thought."

In September of 2018, Montana Chief District Judge Dana Christensen overturned the USFWS' delisting, thus restoring federal protection to the grizzlies. One factor in Christensen's decision, he wrote, was that the delisting agency had not sufficiently taken into account the effect delisting the Yellowstone bears would have on the populations of the other grizzly ecosystems in the contiguous states.

The fight continues over the management of grizzlies in Montana, and it may drag on until natural selection produces a bear smart enough to represent itself in court. Predictably, the USFWS filed an appeal against Christensen's eleventh-hour ruling to the U.S. Ninth Circuit Court of Appeals. Hillary Cooley of the USFWS said that appeal alone would add two years to the process. "We were on track to have a (NCDE delisting) proposal by the end of this calendar year (2018). That's not on track anymore." When Secretary Zinke abruptly resigned at the end of 2018, that only added to the turmoil, although Keith Hammer and other environmentalists know that the delisting efforts of the government agencies will continue, and, armed with science and exhaustive data, Hammer and his colleagues will continue to fight for further protection of Montana's grizzlies.

Meanwhile, the 700 grizzly bears in the Greater Yellowstone Ecosystem, the thousand grizzlies in the Northern Continental Divide Ecosystem, the seventy to eighty bears in the Yaak-Cabinet range and the scattering of renegades in western Montana forests go about their business. In October 2018, a two-year-old male grizzly was captured on the Whitetail golf course in Stevensville, digging up the greens in search of earthworms. The golf course is situated at the edge of the Bitterroot Ecosystem, which is suitable habitat but supposedly contains no grizzlies. The young bear was relocated to the NCDE. Grizzlies continue to push beyond the invisible boundaries of their respective territories, searching for increasingly scarce food, suitable habitat, and other bears. They are claiming more and more of Montana for their own, and one way or another, we are going to have to come to terms with it.

DOWN THE ROAD: THE SEVENTH MONTANA

THE SEVENTH MONTANA IS NOT ON THE MAP. It's the Montana we want to keep, and the Montana that needs to change. It is a tricky time for all seven Montanas. It's becoming harder to protect this treasure of the American West, where people once came to claim their 320 acres and plant the seeds of their lives, the place where so many millions continue to return each year from all over the world for fun and adventure, sometimes deciding to stay for good. As Montana moves forward, answers don't come easy, and the questions are coming faster and louder. If there's one thing we can all agree on, though, it's that Montana deserves our best efforts. Across the state, we're working to effect positive change in different ways, and our agendas are largely determined by our location.

"Every place in the Intermountain West has a lot of challenges," says Ben Lamb, a 36-year-old consultant who works on natural resource issues. "You can view those as insurmountable problems that you'll never overcome, or as opportunities to strive to improve the human condition along the way." In Helena, Lamb works at shaping government policies that protect access to public lands for fishing and hunting, while finding a balance that still allows for judicious use of natural resources. His labors are bearing fruit, as he's seeing some positive results in the efforts to lead Montana away from the environmental damage caused by the extractive industries. "Ten years from now we're going to be looking at some of these issues that we've punted on, like mine remediation. The people of this part of Montana (Gold West Country) look around and see the remnants of these mines and realize you can't drink out of certain water or creeks because of arsenic poisoning or heavy metals leaching out of the Berkeley Pit. And so I think you start to see citizens taking the reins of their future more, rather than leaving it up to corporate entities or the government. Either people will lead and politicians will have to follow, or we decide that ruining our streams and drinking water and wildlife habitat is worth it for one generation's worth of jobs." Forestry and mining aren't necessarily bad things, he says, but we must keep working

Perhaps nowhere more than Butte is an extractive industry's aftermath more evident. Montana's rich natural resources continue to provide jobs and product statewide, but Montana must work hard to balance the need for environmental protections with the economic benefits brought by these industries.

to find ways to allow these traditional industries to thrive without destroying the very landscape that makes Montana so special. It's a fundamental issue not just in Gold West Country, but also in Custer Country, Missouri River Country, and all areas of Montana where oil, natural gas, coal, gold, timber, and other natural resources are still being removed from the land.

In Havre, Pam and Gerry Veis are also contending with damage being inflicted on Montana, but it's people, not the land, that are being torn apart. "The hate has gotten so bad," says Pam, a retired mental health case manager. "It's disheartening. I think it's always been there but now it's so in our face. It's oozing, festering. I guess in order to heal, everything has to be exposed." Endemic racism toward Native Americans

Jay Laber's Blackfeet warrior sculptures stand at the entrance to the reservation near East Glacier.

has been poisoning families and communities for generations in Montana, and in the Veises' neck of the woods, it may be the worst in the state. But Native Americans and non-Natives are starting to see some glimmers of hope, and it's coming from the youngest people within their own families.

"To me, every generation that we have always downplays the greatness of the next generation," says Gerry, an administrator at a local credit union. "These young kids that we have today, their diversity, their closeness as human beings, is better than any generation that's ever existed." The Veises have two children in their thirties, and the internet, he believes, has been the game-changer. "It's a much more diverse outlook than I was afforded."

Pam has high hopes about the generations to come, and about their ability to start closing the racial divide. "I substitute teach these little second and third graders, and maybe half of them are Native, and I just don't see kids seeing color. I really don't. I think it's because of the exposure that they have now and they're just broader-minded." In a state that lacks racial diversity, the connection to the rest of the world provided by the internet will be a crucial factor, she says, adding that learning about one another's cultural heritage is another idea that will go a long way toward achieving mutual respect between Native Americans and non-Natives.

In Missoula, Thurston Elfstrom, 48, agrees that the hope for Montana's future lies in its young people, and his goal as executive director of the Montana Natural History Center (MNHC) is to get kids outside more. "We're running our kids ragged," he says. "We have to give kids more time to be kids. So at the Natural History Center we're mentoring them and teaching them about exploring."

Technology, he says, is a double-edged sword. "You can't get kids off the screens." The same internet that opens up the world to a kid in a remote Montana town can also keep that kid glued to the screen for hours on end. The key is to use the technology to close Montana's vast distances. "We're actually using a green screen-enabled webcam. We're connecting with classrooms in Rapelje and Colstrip, bridging a five-hour drive instantly. We're doing things like using bird- and flower-identification software on smartphones in the field." As technology continues to develop, he says, it will actually help the MNHC become more effective in getting kids outdoors. "Kids are into having fun. They're built to play in the dirt. My hope for Montana down the road is that we've conserved more green space and that we've protected our public lands."

A butterfly alights on one of Montana's wildflowers.

While there's a whiff of optimism for Montana's future in the air, we're certainly not immune to the polarized socio-political atmosphere that has our country more divided than it's been since the Vietnam War. You don't have to look any further than social media to see it, and Krista Fahlgren of Malta fears that we won't be able to move forward at all until we can dial back the hostility. The 43-year-old writer lives in north-central Montana, where the ranchers-versus-environmentalists debate is white-hot. "We are facing real challenges here," she says, "and if we as a people, as a nation, state, and community, can't learn to talk to each other with enough respect to find some common ground, we will be a watered-down version of who we are. We might as well just go hide in the bunker now." She acknowledges that there are no easy solutions, but that doesn't keep her from stepping up to the plate. "I'm just trying to figure out if and what I can do here to make my life work and other lives better."

Fahlgren's truth is our truth. In order to do what's best for all seven Montanas, we have to start by doing what's best for ourselves, and we have to be in it for the long game. The short-sighted actions of the pioneers and speculators who were drawn to Montana by its abundance of natural resources a hundred and fifty years ago left behind scars that we're still dealing with today. For twelve thousand years before that, people in what is now Montana thrived not because they dominated the environment, but because they understood that they were a part of it.

In all six of Montana's regions, the struggle to protect Montana's resources but still profit from them is an inescapable conundrum. Just as there is more to Montana than simply East versus West, there are multiple facets to each region's version of the struggle. There's one available resource, though, that's more valuable than any amount of oil, gold, lumber or other tangible commodity that can be yanked from the ground. It's information. Every Montanan has a stake in its future, and we all deserve to have informed decisions made about how we get there. For one thing, we need to start listening to each other. Those people on the other side of the fence? They're your neighbors. You might not see eye to eye on a lot of issues, but if we listen to each other, stick to the facts, and consider other perspectives outside our own echo chambers, we'll have a better shot at finding workable solutions that will help Montana move into the future while respecting and honoring its past. We'll also find that we have more in common than we realized. When you stop to think about it, there is one important trait that we all share. Whether there are seven Montanas or seven hundred Montanas, we all chose to live our lives under the same big sky.

ABOUT THE AUTHOR

EDNOR THERRIAULT works as a writer, musician and graphic designer who loves to examine life on the fringes. His other books include *Montana Curiosities, Montana Off the Beaten Path* and *Myths and Legends of Yellowstone*, and his writing can be found in *Distinctly Montana, Mountain Outlaw* and other publications. A military brat, Ednor grew up all over the U.S., and eventually settled in Missoula, his father's hometown. He spends as much time as he can traveling the state and learning of its history, its people, and the endless stories that need to be told.

Working under the stage name Bob Wire, Ednor has written, recorded, and released five albums of original music, and opened for such acts as Brad Paisley, James McMurtry and the Bottle Rockets. Guitar in hand, he performs frequently around western Montana. He has two grown children, Hudson and Sophia, and lives in Missoula with his wife Shannon.